ASPECTS
of PSYCHOLOGY

THERAPEUTIC
APPROACHES

LIBRARY AND LEARNING RESOURCES CENTRE
Northern College, Barnsley. S75 3ET

Please return this book by the last date stamped below.

D1332844

NC007 14

ASPECTS of PSYCHOLOGY

THERAPEUTIC APPROACHES to ABNORMAL BEHAVIOUR

RICHARD GROSS & ROB MCILVEEN

Hodder & Stoughton

A MEMBER OF THE HODDER HEADLINE GROUP

Dedication

To all students of Psychology: past, present and future

British Library Cataloguing in Publication Data
A catalogue record for this title is available from the British Library

ISBN 0 340 74905 9

First published 1999
Impression number   10 9 8 7 6 5 4 3 2 1
Year   2003 2002 2001 2000 1999

Typeset by GreenGate Publishing Services, Tonbridge, Kent.
Printed and bound in Great Britain for Hodder and Stoughton Educational, a division of
Hodder Headline plc, 338 Euston Road, London NW1 3BH,
by Cox & Wyman, Reading, Berks

CONTENTS

Preface   vii

Acknowledgements   viii

1 **Therapies based on the medical
   model**   1
   Introduction and overview; Chemotherapy;
   Electroconvulsive therapy; Psychosurgery;
   Conclusions; Summary

2 **Therapies based on the
   psychodynamic model**   18
   Introduction and overview; Psychoanalysis;
   Psychoanalytically oriented psychotherapies;
   Psychodynamic approaches to group therapy;
   Therapies based on the psychodynamic model:
   some issues; Conclusions; Summary

3 **Therapies based on the
   behavioural model**   35
   Introduction and overview; Therapies based on
   classical conditioning: behaviour therapy; Therapies
   based on operant conditioning: behaviour
   modification techniques; Some general comments
   about therapies based on the behavioural model;
   Conclusions; Summary

4 **Therapies based on the cognitive
   model**   53
   Introduction and overview; Bandura's approaches to
   therapy; Ellis' rational–emotive therapy (RET);
   Beck's cognitive restructuring therapy; Attributional
   therapy; Meichenbaum's stress inoculation therapy;
   Some other applications of therapies derived from
   the cognitive model; Conclusions; Summary

5 Therapies based on the humanistic model   **69**

Introduction and overview; Rogers' client- (or person-) centred therapy; Perls' Gestalt therapy; Humanistic approaches to group therapy; Conclusions; Summary

6 Assessing the effectiveness of therapies   **85**

Introduction and overview; Early attempts at assessing therapy's effectiveness; The issue of measurement; Meta-analytic studies; Comparing the relative effectiveness of therapies; Conclusions; Summary

References   **101**

Index   **109**

PREFACE

The *Aspects of Psychology* series aims to provide a short and concise, but detailed and highly accessible, account of selected areas of psychological theory and research.

Therapeutic Approaches to Abnormal Behaviour consists of 6 chapters. Chapters 1–5 critically consider five major approaches to the treatment of abnormal behaviour, each one being based on a model of abnormality: namely, the medical, psychodynamic, behavioural, cognitive and humanistic. The final chapter examines the issue of how the effectiveness of therapies can be assessed.

For the purposes of revision, we have included detailed summaries of the material presented in each chapter. Instead of a separate glossary, for easy reference the Index contains page numbers in **bold** which refer to definitions and main explanations of particular concepts.

ACKNOWLEDGEMENTS

We would like to thank Dave Mackin, Anna Churchman and Denise Stewart at GreenGate Publishing for their swift and efficient preparation of the text. Thanks also to Greig Aitken at Hodder for all his hard work in coordinating this project (we hope it's the first of many!), and to Tim Gregson-Williams for his usual help and support.

Picture Credits

The publishers would like to thank the following for permission to reproduce photographs and other illustrations in this book:

p.9 (Fig 1.1), Science Photo Library, Will and Deni Mcintyre; p.21 (Fig 2.1), The Telegraph Photo Library; p.37 (Fig 3.1), Colorific/ Mark Richards/ Dot Pictures; p.91 (Fig 6.1), The Johns Hopkins University Press from Smith, M.L. *et al.* (1980) *The Benefits of Psychotherapy* 1990 The Johns Hopkins University Press.

Every effort has been made to obtain necessary permission with reference to copyright material. The publishers apologise if inadvertently any sources remain unacknowledged and will be glad to make the necessary arrangements at the earliest opportunity.

THERAPIES BASED ON THE MEDICAL MODEL

Introduction and overview

The medical model views mental disorders as being caused largely, if not exclusively, by physical factors. As a result, the medical model's favoured therapeutic approaches are physical, and collectively known as *somatic therapy*. The early and middle parts of the twentieth century saw the introduction of a variety of extraordinary treatments for mental disorders, whose names conjure up disturbing images of what they involved (David, 1994). These include *carbon dioxide inhalation therapy, nitrogen shock therapy, narcosis therapy, insulin coma therapy* and *malaria therapy*.

Although many somatic therapies have been abandoned, three are still used (and their names too may conjure up disturbing images). These are *chemotherapy, electroconvulsive therapy* and *psychosurgery*. This chapter describes these therapies and considers some of the issues surrounding their use.

Chemotherapy

The use of *drugs* to treat mental disorders has been the most influential of the currently used somatic therapies. Indeed, according to SANE (1993), a quarter of all medications prescribed in Britain through the National Health Service are *psychotherapeutic* drugs. The three main types of drug are *neuroleptics, antidepressants* and *antimanics*, and *anxiolytics*.

Neuroleptics

Neuroleptics were the forerunners of the 'drug revolution' in the treatment of mental disorders. These were introduced in the 1950s following the accidental discovery that they calmed psychotic individuals. Since they lessened the need for the physical restraint (such as straitjackets) of seriously disturbed individuals, they were seen as a great advance in treatment. Neuroleptics are also known as *major tranquillisers*, although this term is misleading because they generally tranquillise without impairing consciousness. The term *antipsychotics* is also used to describe them, because they are mainly used to treat schizophrenia and other severe disorders, such as mania and amphetamine abuse.

Box 1.1 *The neuroleptic drugs*

Examples: The most widely used group are the *phenothiazines* and include *chlorpromazine* (marketed under the trade names *Thorazine* and *Largactil*). The *butyrophenone* group includes haloperidol (*Haldol*) and *droperidol* (*Droleptan*). One of the more recent neuroleptics is *clozapine* (*Clozaril*), a member of the dibezazepines group, which was developed to avoid the side-effects (see below) of the phenothiazines.

Mode of action: Most neuroleptics block D2 *dopamine* receptors in the brain, with the result that dopamine cannot excite post-synaptic receptors. Neuroleptics also inhibit the functioning of the hypothalamus (which contains dopamine secreting neurons). The hypothalamus plays a role in arousal, and neuroleptic drugs prevent arousal signals from reaching higher brain regions. Rather than blocking D2 receptors, clozapine blocks D4 receptors, and for that reason is known as an *atypical* neuroleptic.

Side-effects: Of many that have been reported, the more extreme include blurred vision, *neuroleptic malignant syndrome* (which produces delirium, coma and death) and *extrapyramidal symptoms*. These consist of *akathisia* (restlessness), *dystonia* (abnormal body movements, one of which is known as the 'Thorazine shuffle'), and *tardive dyskinesia*. Tardive (late onset) dyskinesia (movement disorder) is an irreversible condition resembling Parkinson's disease. Some side-effects can be controlled by the use of other drugs such as *procyclidine* (*Kemadrin*).

Attempts to limit side-effects include *targeted strategies* or *drug holidays*, in which the drugs are discontinued during periods of remission and reinstituted when early signs of relapse occur. *Agranulocytosis* (a decrease in the number of infection-fighting white blood cells) is a side-effect of clozapine and some other neuroleptics. It occurs in about two per cent of users, and is potentially fatal. Blood

---

tests must be given on a regular basis. When the cell count drops too low, the drug's use must be permanently discontinued. Newer neuroleptics such as *risperidone (Risperdal)* may avoid many of the side-effects described above (NSF, 1994). *Olanzapine*, which has a similar action to clozapine but without the haematological complications, is marketed under the trade name Zyprexa (BNF, 1997).

Typical neuroleptics are effective in reducing schizophrenia's *positive* symptoms (delusions, hallucinations and thought disorder), and allow other therapies to be used when the symptoms are in remission. However, some people fail to respond to the drugs, especially those displaying *negative* symptoms (decreased speech, lack of drive, diminished social interaction, and loss of emotional response), such as apathy and withdrawal. Although *atypical* neuroleptics may treat negative symptoms, antipsychotic drugs do not cure schizophrenia, but reduce its prominent symptoms (Hutton, 1998). Relapse occurs after several weeks if the drugs are stopped. Additionally, neuroleptics are of little value in treating social incapacity and other difficulties in adjusting to life outside the therapeutic setting. As a result, relapse is common (Green, 1996).

Antidepressants and antimanics

Antidepressants are classified as *stimulants* and were also introduced in the 1950s. As well as treating depression, they have been used in the treatment of anxiety, agoraphobia, obsessive–compulsive disorder and eating disorders (Hamilton & Timmons, 1995).

Box 1.2 *Antidepressants*

Examples: The *monoamine oxidase inhibitor* (MAOI) group includes *phenelzine* (marketed under the trade name *Nardil*). The *tricyclic* group includes *imipramine (Tofranil)*. The *tetracyclic* group includes *fluoxetine (Prozac)*. Because of their mode of action (see below), the tetracyclics are also known as *selective serotonin re-uptake inhibitors* (SSRIs).

Mode of action: MAOIs are so called because they inhibit (or block) the uptake of the enzyme that deactivates *noradrenaline* and *serotonin*. Thus, they are believed to act directly on these neurotransmitters. The tricyclic group prevents the re-uptake of noradrenaline and serotonin by the cells that released them, making these neurotransmitters more likely to reach receptor sites. The tetracyclics block the action of an enzyme that removes serotonin from the synapses between neurons (hence serotonin levels are elevated).

Side-effects: MAOIs require adherence to a special diet. Amine-rich food (such as some cheeses, pickled herrings and yeast extracts) must be avoided. Failure to do so results in the accumulation of amines, which causes cerebral haemorrhage. Both MAOIs and the tricyclics are associated with cardiac arrhythmias and heart block, dry mouth, blurred vision and urinary retention. Tetracyclic drugs like Prozac are also not free from serious side-effects, including impairment of sexual function (Breggin, 1996) and abnormal aggression (Cornwell, 1996). The most recent antidepressants include *reboxetine* (*Edronax*), which exerts its effects exclusively on noradrenaline (Lemonick, 1997).

None of the antidepressants identified in Box 1.2 exerts immediate effects (Stevenson & Baker, 1996). For example, *tricyclics* can take up to four weeks before a noticeable change in behaviour is observed (and with individuals who are so depressed that they are contemplating suicide, this is clearly a drawback). However, when mood improves, psychological therapies can be used to try and get at the root of the depression. MAOIs are generally less effective than tricyclics, and because of dietary requirements and the fact that they have more side-effects than tricyclics, MAOIs are the least preferred antidepressant drug.

Prozac, an SSRI antidepressant, was introduced in 1987. It has been termed the 'happy pill' and its users 'the happy, shiny people'. Because Prozac was believed to have fewer side-effects than the tricyclics, it has been widely prescribed as a treatment for depression. The claim that Prozac can increase happiness and create a 'more interesting personality' has produced astonishing sales. More than 15 million people worldwide take the drug, including 500,000 in Britain (Costello *et al.*, 1995). In 1996, American *children* aged between six and 18 received 735,000 prescriptions for Prozac and other SSRIs (Laurence, 1997).

Although antidepressants are effective when used in the short term with severe depression, they are not useful on a long-term basis. Indeed, they do not alleviate depression in all people, and controlled studies suggest their effectiveness is no greater than psychotherapy and cognitive therapy (NIMH, 1987). As Box 1.2 illustrates, one side-effect (especially of the tricyclics) is *urinary retention*. Controversially, this has been used to treat *nocturnal enuresis* (bedwetting) in children, even when other simple measures have not been tried.

Lithium carbonate was approved as an antimanic drug in 1970, but was actually first used in the mid-nineteenth century for *gouty mania* (Garrod, 1859). It is used to treat both bipolar disorder (depression and mania occurring in conjunction, or mania alone) and unipolar disorder (depression only). Lithium salts (such as *lithium carbonate* and *lithium citrate*) flatten out cycles of manic behaviour. Once the manic phase in bipolar disorder has been eliminated, the depressed phase does not return. Lithium salts appear to be 'miracle drugs', in that within two weeks of taking them, 70–80 per cent of manic individuals show an improvement in mood.

Box 1.3 *Antimanics*

Examples: The inorganic salts lithium carbonate and lithium citrate are marketed under a variety of trade names including *Camoclit* and *Liskanum* (both lithium carbonate) and *Litarex* and *Piradel* (both lithium citrate).

Mode of action: By increasing the re-uptake of *noradrenaline* and *serotonin*, it is believed that lithium carbonate decreases their availability at various synaptic sites.

Side-effects: These include depressed reactions, hand tremors, dry mouth, weight gain, impaired memory and kidney poisoning. If lithium becomes too concentrated in the bloodstream, side effects include nausea, diarrhoea and, at very high levels, coma and death. As a result, users' blood is regularly checked.

Anxiolytics

These are classified as *depressants* and are also known as *anti-anxiety drugs* or *minor tranquillisers*. Anxiety was first treated with synthetic *barbiturates* (such as *phenobarbitol*). However, because of their side-effects and the introduction of other anxiolytic drugs, their use gradually declined. Anxiolytics are used to reduce anxiety and tension in people whose disturbances are not severe enough to warrant hospitalisation. The drugs are effective in reducing the symptoms of generalised anxiety disorder (GAD), especially when used in the short term and in combination with psychological therapies. They are also used to combat withdrawal symptoms associated with opiate and alcohol addiction. However, anxiolytics are of little use in treating the anxiety that occurs in sudden, spontaneous panic attacks.

Box 1.4 *Anxiolytics*

Examples: The *propanediol* group includes *meprobamate* (marketed under the trade name *Miltown*). The *benzodiazepine* group includes *chlordiazepoxide* (*Librium*) and *diazepam* (*Valium*).
Mode of action: Their general effect is to depress CNS activity, which causes a decrease in activity of the sympathetic branch of the ANS. This produces decreased heart and respiration rate and reduces feelings of nervousness and tension. Since benzodiazepine receptor sites exist in the brain, that group might exert their effect by mimicking or blocking a naturally occurring substance yet to be discovered.
Side-effects: These include drowsiness, lethargy, tolerance, dependence, withdrawal (manifested as tremors and convulsions) and toxicity. *Rebound anxiety* (anxiety which is even more intense than

that originally experienced) can occur when their use is stopped. Rebound anxiety may be physiological or psychological in origin. Newer anxiolytics (such as *Busparin* and *Zopiclone*) seem to be as effective as established anxiolytics, although unpleasant side-effects have also been reported with them.

The term *minor tranquillisers* might suggest that anxiolytic drugs are 'safe'. However, one of their dangers is that overdose can lead to death, especially when taken with alcohol. As Box 1.4 shows, anxiolytics also produce addiction. Although it is generally agreed that anxiolytic use should be limited to people whose anxiety is clearly handicapping their work, leisure and family relationships, they are all too commonly prescribed. Indeed, Valium is the most prescribed of all drugs. An astonishing 8000 tons of *benzodiazepines* were consumed in the United States alone in 1977, and 21 million prescriptions issued in Britain alone in 1989 (Rassool & Winnington, 1993). As with other drugs, their use with children (to relieve acute anxiety and related insomnia caused by fear) is controversial, and the use of benzodiazepines during pregnancy has been linked with vascular and limb malformations in the offspring (MacDonald, 1996).

Electroconvulsive therapy

Sakel (1933, cited in Fink, 1984) found that inducing a hypo-glycaemic coma by means of insulin seemed to be effective in treating certain psychoses. Later, von Meduna claimed that schiz-ophrenia and epilepsy were *biologically incompatible*, that is, schizophrenia rarely occurred in epilepsy and vice versa. Drawing on his observation that psychotic individuals prone to epilepsy showed less severe symptoms following an epileptic fit, von Meduna advocated inducing major epileptiform fits in psychotics in order to 'drive out' and hence 'cure' their schizophrenia.

Von Meduna used *Cardiazol*, a cerebral stimulant, to induce the epileptic fit. However, this method was unsatisfactory, not least because it induced feelings of impending death during the conscious phase of its action! Various alternatives were tried until, after visiting an abattoir and seeing animals rendered unconscious by means of electric shocks, Cerletti and Bini (Bini, 1938) advocated passing an electric current across the temples to induce an epileptic fit. Although there have been refinements to Cerletti and Bini's original procedures, *electroconvulsive therapy* (ECT) is still administered in essentially the same way.

Box 1.5　*The procedures used in ECT*

Following a full physical examination (necessary because heart conditions, chest diseases and peptic ulcers can be accentuated by ECT), the person is required to fast for three to four hours prior to treatment and empty the bladder immediately before treatment. Whilst being psychologically prepared, dentures, rings and other metallic objects are removed and a loose-fitting gown worn.

Forty-five to sixty minutes before treatment, an *atropine sulphate* injection is given. This prevents the heart's normal rhythm from being disturbed and inhibits the secretion of mucus and saliva. An anxiolytic drug may also be given if a person is particularly apprehensive. With the person lying supine, head supported by a pillow, a short-acting anaesthetic followed by a muscle relaxant is given, the latter ensuring that a reduced convulsion will occur. Oxygen is given before and after treatment, and a mouth gag is applied to prevent the tongue or lips being bitten.

In *bilateral* ECT, saline-soaked lint-covered electrodes are attached to each temple. In *unilateral* ECT, two electrodes are attached to the temple and mastoid region of the non-dominant cerebral hemisphere. With the chin held still, a current of around 200 milliamps, flowing at 110 volts, is passed from one electrode to another for a brief period (around 0.5–4 seconds).

Because of the use of muscle relaxants, the only observable sign of the fit is a slight twitching of the eyelids, facial muscles, and toes. When the convulsion is complete and the jaw relaxed, an airway is inserted into the mouth, and oxygen given until breathing resumes unaided. The person is turned into the left lateral position, head on the side, and is carefully observed until the effects of the muscle relaxant and anaesthetic have worn off and recovery is complete.

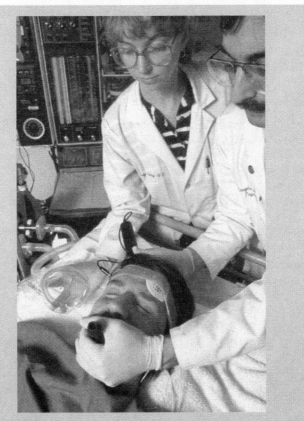

Figure 1.1 *ECT as it is carried out today. Despite the technical improvements, ECT is a highly controversial treatment*

Typically, a number of ECT treatments occurring over several weeks will be administered, the amount being gauged by the individual's response (Freeman, 1995). Although originally used to treat schizophrenia, ECT's usefulness with that disorder has been seriously questioned, and today it is primarily used to treat severe depression, bipolar disorder and certain obsessive–compulsive disorders. In Britain, around 20,000 people a year undergo ECT (Johnston, 1996). According to Wesseley (1993),

ECT is 'highly effective' in the treatment of severe depression and particularly useful with those who harbour suicidal feelings, because its effects are immediate (unlike the antidepressant drugs: see page 4).

Box 1.6 *Explaining ECT's effectiveness*

Whilst ECT's effectiveness in certain disorders is beyond dispute, its use has been questioned on the grounds that it is not known why the beneficial effects occur (Benton, 1981). It might be due to the *anterograde* and *retrograde amnesia* that occur as a side-effect. However, unilateral ECT (see Box 1.5), which minimises memory disruption, is also effective in reducing depression. As a result, a 'memory loss' theory is unlikely to be true.

Given ECT's nature and the negative publicity it has received, a person might deny his or her symptoms to avoid the 'punishment' the therapy is perceived as being, which extinguishes the abnormal behaviour. This possibility has been tested by applying *sub-convulsive shocks*. However, these do not seem to be beneficial and, since they are as unpleasant as convulsive shocks, a 'punishment' theory account is also unlikely to be true.

The most plausible account of ECT's effectiveness is that it produces a variety of *biochemical changes* in the brain which are greater than those produced by antidepressant drugs. However, many physiological changes occur when ECT is administered, and it is difficult to establish which of these are important. Since ECT appears to be most effective in the treatment of depression, and since both noradrenaline and serotonin have been strongly implicated in that disorder, it is most likely that these neurotransmitters are affected (Lilienfeld, 1995).

ECT has also been criticised on ethical grounds. Indeed, in 1982, it was outlawed in Berkeley, California by voter referendum, and its use was punishable by a fine of up to $500 and six months in jail. As noted earlier, ECT has a negative public image deriving from horrific descriptions in books and films. Some of its opponents have described the therapy as being 'about as scientific as kicking a television set because it is not working' (Heather, 1976).

Certainly, the primitive methods once used were associated with bruises and bone fractures (a consequence of the restraint used by nursing staff during the convulsion), and with pain when an individual failed to lose consciousness during the treatment. However, the use of muscle relaxants minimises the possibility of fractures, and anaesthetics rule out the possibility of the individual being conscious during treatment (see Box 1.5).

Yet whilst ECT is now considered to be a 'low-risk' therapeutic procedure, Breggin (1979) has argued that brain damage can occur following its administration (at least in non-humans sacrificed immediately after receiving ECT). Breggin has also pointed out that whilst ECT is typically seen as a treatment of 'last resort', which should be preceded by a careful assessment of the costs and benefits for a particular individual, such assessments are not always routine. Although this may be true in the United States, under Section 58 of the Mental Health Act (1983), ECT's use in Britain requires an individual's consent or a second medical opinion before it can be administered.

Psychosurgery

Psychosurgery refers to surgical procedures that are performed on the brain to treat mental disorders. The term is properly used when the intention is to *purposely* alter psychological functioning. Thus, whilst removing a brain tumour might affect a person's behaviour, it would not constitute a psychosurgical procedure.

Psychosurgical techniques, albeit primitive ones, have been carried out for a long time. In medieval times, psychosurgery involved 'cutting the stone of folly' from the brains of those considered to be 'mad'. Modern psychosurgical techniques can be traced to the Second International Neurological Conference held in London in 1935, when Jacobsen reported the effects of removing the pre-frontal areas (the forwardmost portion) of the frontal lobes in chimpanzees. The procedure apparently abolished the violent outbursts some of the chimpanzees had been prone to.

In the audience was Moniz, a Portugese neuropsychiatrist. Moniz was sufficiently impressed by Jacobsen's findings to persuade a colleague, Lima, to carry out surgical procedures on the frontal lobes of schizophrenics and other disturbed individuals in an attempt to reduce their aggressive behaviour. The procedure involved severing the neural connections between the pre-frontal areas and the hypothalamus and thalamus, the rationale being that thought (mediated by the cortex) would be disconnected from emotion (mediated by lower brain centres).

The *leucotomy* or *pre-frontal lobotomy* seemed to be successful in reducing aggressive behaviour in unmanageable patients. The original 'apple corer' technique involved drilling a hole through the skull covering on each side of the head and then inserting a blunt instrument which was rotated in a vertical arc. This procedure followed the unsuccessful technique of injecting alcohol to destroy areas of frontal lobe brain tissue. Moniz originally used the technique on schizophrenics and people who were compulsive and anxiety-ridden. After a year, a 70 per cent 'cure' rate was claimed by Moniz and Lima.

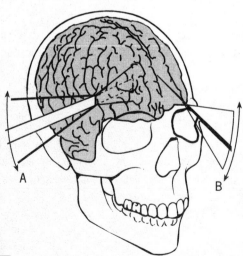

Figure 1.2 *The 'apple corer' technique originally used by Moniz and Lima*

Also at the 1935 conference was Freeman, a neurologist who was not trained as a surgeon. Freeman & Watts (1942) developed and popularised the 'standard' pre-frontal lobotomy. In the absence of alternative therapeutic techniques, and with the seemingly high success rate claimed by Moniz and others, the operation became extremely common. Estimates vary as to the number of operations performed in the United States following Freeman and Watts' pioneering work. Kalinowsky (1975) puts it at around 40,000, whilst Valenstein's (1980) estimate is 25,000. Although not surgically trained, Freeman developed his own psychosurgical technique called the *transorbital lobotomy*.

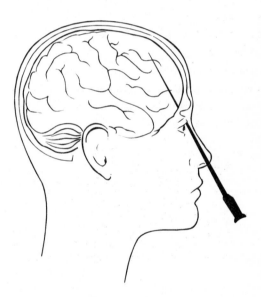

Figure 1.3   *The transorbital lobotomy*

Psychosurgery was largely abandoned in the late 1950s following the introduction of the psychotherapeutic drugs, and various other reasons.

Box 1.7   *Some reasons for the abandonment of psychosurgery*

Lack of scientific basis: The theoretical rationale for Moniz's oper-ation was vague and misguided, with researchers not *entirely* clear why beneficial effects should occur. Indeed, David (1994) has ques-tioned whether even now knowledge of the frontal lobes (or what he calls 'frontal lobology') is anything more than 'psychiatry's new pseudoscience'. Moniz's reports of success were also exaggerated, and whilst he was awarded the Nobel prize for medicine in 1949 'for his discovery of the therapeutic value of leucotomy in the treat-ment of some psychoses', it is ironic that he was shot and paralysed by a patient on whom he had performed a lobotomy! (Valenstein, 1990).

Consistency and irreversibility: Psychosurgery produces incon-sistent outcomes. Behaviour change occurs in some individuals but not others, though who will be affected, and how, is difficult to pre-dict. Psychosurgical procedures cannot be reversed.

Side-effects: Some of the severe and permanent side-effects asso-ciated with psychosurgery are (in no particular order):

apathy; impaired judgement; reduced creativity; epileptic-type seizures; severe blunting of emotions; intellectual impairments; hyperactivity; distractability; impaired learning ability; overeat-ing; partial paralysis; memory loss; personal slovenliness; childlike behaviour; indifference to others; death.

Lack of evaluation: One surgeon noted that the *cingulotomy* (see below) produces 'little or no changes in intellectual and discrimina-tive ability' using the ability to knit after the operation as the criterion for change (Winter, 1972).

Consent: Psychosurgical techniques were routinely used with peo-ple who could not give their consent to the operation. However, Section 58 of the revised Mental Health Act in Britain introduced stringent provisions regarding information to those referred for psychosurgery and their consent to treatment (Rappaport, 1992).

Given the reasons identified above, it is perhaps surprising to learn that, although controversial, psychosurgery is still per-formed today. However, it is very much a treatment of last resort used only when other treatment methods have failed. It is also occasionally used for pain control in the terminally ill.

According to Snaith (1994), over 20 operations a year are conducted in Britain.

Modern lobotomies (*capsulotomies*) involve cutting two tiny holes in the forehead which allow radioactive electrodes to be inserted into the frontal lobe to destroy tissue by means of beta rays. Other psychosurgical techniques involve the destruction of small amounts of tissue in precisely located areas of the brain using a computer controlled electrode which is heated to 68°C. For example, the *tractotomy* interrupts the neural pathways between the limbic system and hypothalamus, in the hope of alleviating depression.

Psychosurgical techniques reduce the risk of suicide in severe depression from 15 per cent to one per cent (Verkaik, 1995). The *cingulotomy* cuts the cingulum bundle (a small bundle of nerve fibres connecting the pre-frontal cortex with parts of the limbic system). This is used to treat obsessive–compulsive disorder, and evidently does so effectively (Hay *et al.*, 1993).

Even more controversial than ECT, psychosugery continues to have a negative image amongst both professionals and the public (Davison & Neale, 1994). However, according to Valenstein (1973):

> **'There are certainly no grounds for either the position that all psychosurgery necessarily reduces all people to a 'vegetable status' or that it has a high probability of producing miraculous cures. The truth, even if somewhat wishy-washy, lies in between these extreme positions'.**

Conclusions

Somatic therapies, which derive from the medical model, have long been used to treat abnormal behaviour. This chapter has described and evaluated three somatic approaches to therapy. Although controversial, they continue to be used today in the treatment of mental disorders.

Summary

- **Somatic approaches** are favoured by the medical model, and include **chemotherapy**, **electroconvulsive therapy** (ECT) and **psychosurgery**. The most influential somatic approach is chemotherapy. Three main types of psychotherapeutic drug are the **neuroleptics**, **antidepressants** and **antimanics**, and **anxiolytics**.

- The neuroleptics (**major tranquillisers** or **antipsychotics**) are mainly used to treat schizophrenia, mania and amphetamine abuse. Most exert their effects by blocking D2 dopamine receptors, whilst atypical neuroleptics act on D4 receptors. Although effective, neuroleptics have many unpleasant and sometimes permanent side-effects. These include **neuroleptic malignant syndrome** and **extrapyramidal symptoms**.

- Neuroleptics reduce schizophrenia's **positive** symptoms, but are less effective with its **negative** symptoms. They do not cure schizophrenia and are of little value in treating social incapacity and other difficulties in adjusting to life in the outside world. As a result, relapse is common.

- **Antidepressants** are used to treat several disorders apart from depression. **Selective serotonin reuptake inhibitors** (SSRIs) are widely accepted as being more beneficial than **monoamine oxidase inhibitors** (MAOIs) and **tricyclics**. SSRIs affect serotonin levels, whilst MAOIs and tricylcics influence both serotonin and noradrenaline. Newer antidepressants (e.g. **reboxetine**) only influence noradrenaline.

- Antidepressants take time to exert their effects, which limits their use with people who are suicidally depressed. Whilst they may be useful in the short-term, they are not useful on a long-term basis. All are associated with unpleasant side-effects, and some are controversially used to treat other problems (such as bedwetting).

- Salts of the metal lithium (lithium carbonate and lithium citrate) are used to treat both bipolar and unipolar disorders.

Within two weeks of taking them, 70–80 per cent of manic individuals show an improvement in mood. They increase the re-uptake of noradrenaline and serotonin. However, unpleasant side-effects are also associated with their use.

- **Anxiolytic drugs** (**anti-anxiety drugs** or **minor tranquillisers**) depress CNS activity, producing a decrease in activity in the sympathetic branch of the ANS. Some may mimic or block naturally occurring brain substances. Side-effects include **rebound anxiety**. They also produce **addiction**. Despite this, their use is still widespread.

- ECT is used to treat depression, bipolar disorder, and certain obsessive–compulsive disorders. Typically, several treatments will be administered over a number of weeks. Although it is not known exactly why ECT is effective, the most plausible theory attributes its effectiveness to **biochemical changes** in the brain. Because it is not known how it works, ECT continues to be controversial.

- **Psychosurgery** involves performing surgical procedures on the brain to purposely alter psychological functioning. Originally, the **leucotomy/pre-frontal lobotomy** was used with aggressive schizophrenics, as was the **transorbital lobotomy**. At least 25,000 psychosurgical operations were performed in the United States alone.

- Psychosurgery was largely abandoned in the 1950s, following the introduction of psychotherapeutic drugs. Operations often lacked a sound theoretical rationale, did not produce consistent effects, and were associated with many side-effects. However, some surgical procedures are still performed, although only as a last resort. Around 20 operations are performed annually in Britain.

THERAPIES BASED ON THE PSYCHODYNAMIC MODEL

2 Introduction and overview

The psychodynamic model sees mental disorders as stemming from the demands of the *id* and/or the *superego*. If the *ego* is too weak to cope with these, it defends itself by repressing them into the unconscious. However, the conflicts do not disappear, but find expression through behaviour (and this is the disorder a person experiences).

For Freud (1894), it is not enough to change a person's present behaviours. To bring about a permanent cure, the problems giving rise to the behaviours must also be changed. Because psychological problems have their origins in events that occurred earlier in life, Freud did not see present problems as the *psychoanalyst's* domain, because people will already have received sympathy and advice from family and friends. If such support was going to help, it would have done so already, and there would be no need for a psychoanalyst to be consulted.

According to Eisenberg (1995), there was a time 'when psychoanalysis was the only game in town'. However, whilst there are more than 400 psychotherapies (Holmes, 1996), the popularity of *psychodynamic* approaches (those based on psychoanalysis) has declined over the years. For example, between 1961 and 1982, the proportion of therapists identifying themselves as psychoanalysts dropped from 41 to 14 per cent (Smith, 1982). Nonetheless, therapies based on the psychodynamic model are 'one of Britain's most recession-proof industries' (Laurance, 1993), and more than 100,000 people are currently receiving some form of psychodynamically-based therapy. This chapter examines the processes involved in Freudian *psychoanalysis* and briefly considers some of the therapeutic variations on it.

Psychoanalysis

The purpose of *psychoanalysis* is to uncover the unconscious conflicts responsible for an individual's mental disorder. In Freud's words, psychoanalysis aims to 'drain the psychic abscess' and 'make the unconscious conscious'. The first step is thus to bring the conflicts into consciousness. Ultimately, this helps the *analysand* (the person undergoing psychoanalysis) to gain *insight* or conscious awareness of the repressed conflicts. The rationale is that once a person understands the reason for a behaviour, the ego can deal more effectively with it and resolve the conflict.

Techniques used in psychoanalysis

Hypnosis

Ordinarily, the ego's defence mechanisms repress certain thoughts. As a result, bringing the unconscious into consciousness is difficult. Freud and his followers devised several methods to achieve this. Originally, Freud used *hypnosis*. This seemed to allow analysands to break through to things they were otherwise unaware of. However, Freud abandoned hypnosis, because some of his analysands denied the accuracy of what they had revealed during it, whilst others found their revelations to be premature and painful.

Dream interpretation

Freud believed that the content of dreams is determined by unconscious processes as well as by the day's 'residues'. Unconscious impulses are expressed in dreams as a form of *wish fulfilment*. Freud believed dreams to be 'the royal road to the unconscious' and a rich source of information about hidden aspects of personality. Things that happened during the day evoked repressed childhood memories and desires. However, because some desires are too disturbing for an individual to face, even when asleep, these are expressed in symbolic form (the dream's *manifest content*). It is the analyst's task to unravel its hidden meaning (the dream's *latent content*).

Interpreting faulty actions and physiological cues

Two other methods used by psychoanalysts are the *interpretation of faulty actions* (or *parapraxes*) and the *interpretation of physiological cues*. Freud saw what others have called *Freudian slips* as a route to the unconscious, because the errors and mistakes we make in everyday life are unconscious thoughts finding their way into consciousness. Freud believed that repressed material could find expression through behaviour which is beyond conscious control, such as erroneous actions, forgetfulness and slips of the tongue and pen. The interpretation of physiological cues is used in conjunction with other methods. Blushing or pallor, and changes in the timbre of a person's voice, can all provide a useful indication of the unconscious significance of ideas touched on in therapy.

Free association

The most widely used technique in psychoanalysis is *free association*. In this, the analysand lies on a comfortable couch so that the analyst cannot be seen (which prevents the latter from distracting the former and interfering with concentration). The analysand is encouraged to say whatever comes to mind, no matter how trivial or frivolous it might seem. Freud called this the *basic rule* of psychoanalysis. He believed that the ego ordinarily acts as a censor, preventing threatening unconscious impulses from entering consciousness. By free-associating, the censor could be 'bypassed'. Although free association is the most widely used technique, it takes several sessions before analysands 'open up'.

Box 2.1 *Introducing an analysand to free association*

In ordinary conversation, you usually try to keep a connecting thread running through your remarks, excluding any intrusive ideas or side issues so as not to wander too far from the point, and rightly so. But in this case, you must talk differently. As you talk, various thoughts will occur to you which you would like to ignore because

---

of certain criticisms and objections. You will be tempted to think, 'that is irrelevant or unimportant or nonsensical,' and to avoid saying it. Do not give in to such criticism. Report such thoughts in spite of your wish not to do so. Later, the reason for this injunction, the only one you have to follow, will become clear. Report whatever goes through your mind. Pretend that you are a traveller, describing to someone beside you the changing views which you see outside the train window.
(From Ford & Urban, 1963)

During analysis, the analyst remains '*anonymous*' and does not express emotion or evaluate the analysand's attitudes. The analyst does not reveal information about him- or herself, since whilst the analyst needs to learn a great deal about the analysand, the reverse is not true. This form of interaction ensures that the analysand does not form a close, personal relationship with the analyst, but views him or her purely as an 'anonymous and ambiguous stimulus'. Whilst the analysand free-associates, the analyst acts as a sort of *sounding board*, often repeating and clarifying what the analysand has said. Thus, the analysand tells a story and the analyst helps interpret it in terms of repressed conflicts and feelings.

Figure 2.1 *During psychoanalysis, the analysand usually reclines on a couch, while the analyst sits behind to avoid distracting the analysand. Although the analyst traditionally plays a passive role, occasionally he or she will offer an interpretation to help the analysand reach an insight*

The main form of communication between the analyst and analysand is the analyst's *interpretive comments*. Sometimes, the analyst may need to draw attention to the analysand's *resistances*. Freud believed that what analysands do *not* say is as important as what they do say. During free association, analysands may express an unwillingness to discuss freely some aspects of their lives. For example, they may disrupt the session, change the subject whenever a particular topic comes up, joke about something as though it was unimportant, arrive late for a session, or perhaps miss it altogether.

Box 2.2 *Freud's description of resistance*

The analysand endeavours in every sort of way to extricate himself from [the rule of free association]. At one moment he declares that nothing occurs to him, at the next that so many things are crowding in on him that he cannot get hold of anything. Presently we observe with pained astonishment that he has given way first to one and then to another critical objection; he betrays this to us by the long pauses that he introduces into his remarks. He then admits that there is something he really cannot say – he would be ashamed to; and he allows this reason to prevail against his promise. Or he says that something has occurred to him, but it concerns another person and not himself and is therefore exempt from being reported. Or, what has now occurred to him is really too unimportant, too silly and senseless; I cannot possibly have meant him to enter into thoughts like that. So it goes on in innumerable variations.
(From Freud, 1894)

Freud saw resistance as natural, because it is painful to bring unconscious conflicts into conscious awareness. It also indicates that the analyst is getting close to the source of the problem and that the unconscious is struggling to avoid 'giving up its secrets'. Although resistance hinders therapy, it provides useful information for both analysand and analyst in the form of clues about the repressed conflict's nature.

As therapy progresses, analysts may *privately deduce* the nature of what is behind the analysand's statements and attempt to generate further associations. For example, the analysand may apologise for saying something believed to be trivial. The analyst tells the analysand that what appears trivial might relate to something important. By appropriately timing this intervention, significant new associations may result. The analyst does not suggest what is important in what the analysand has said. The goal is to help the analysand discover this him- or herself.

Box 2.3 *Confrontation and reconstruction*

As therapy continues, the analyst may try to explain the analysand's behaviour in a way which is new to him or her. For example, analysands may be informed that their anger does not come from where they think it does, but rather that they are angry because the analyst reminds them of someone. In *confrontation*, the analyst tells the analysand exactly what is being revealed in the free associations. In *reconstruction*, the analyst provides hypothetical historical statements of hitherto buried fragments of the analysand's past. For example, the analysand may be told that the anger is a repetition of feelings experienced as a child and that the analyst stands for the objects of that anger.

Transference

Once interpretation is complete and the unconscious conflict has been brought into consciousness, the analyst and the analysand repeat and 'live out' the conflict. The associated feelings which have been repressed for so long then become available for 'manipulation' by the analyst. Freud called this process *transference* or *transference neurosis*. In it, the original source of the conflict is displaced onto the analyst, who now becomes the object of the analysand's emotional responses (see Box 2.3). Depending on the conflict's nature, the feelings may be positive and loving or negative and hostile. By exploring the transference relationship, psychoanalysis assumes that unconscious conflicts can be brought out into the open, understood and resolved. According to Thomas (1990):

'Over the years, it has become increasingly clear to practising analysts that the process of transference ... is one of the most important tools they have. It has become so central to theory and practice that many, though not all, analysts believe that making interpretations about transference is what distinguishes psychoanalysis from other forms of psychotherapy. When attention is focused on the transference and what is happening in the here and now, the historical reconstruction of childhood events and the search for the childhood origins of conflicts may take second place'.

Box 2.4   *Countertransference*

Freud discovered that transference operated in both directions and that he could transfer his own feelings onto his analysands. A male analysand, for example, could be viewed as a 'rebellious son'. Freud called the placing of clients into his own life *countertransference*. To avoid displacing their own repressed childhood feelings and wishes onto their patients, analysts undergo a *training analysis*. This permits them to understand their own conflicts and motivations, so they become *opaque* concerning their own behaviours and feelings to avoid countertransference with their analysands.

Whether the avoidance of countertransference is absolutely necessary is, however, debatable. As Thomas (1990) has observed:

'In Freud's time, countertransference feelings were considered to be a failing on the part of the analyst. These feelings were to be controlled absolutely. Now, countertransference is considered an unavoidable outcome of the analytic process, irrespective of how well prepared the analyst is by analytic training and its years of required personal analysis ... most modern analysts are trained to observe their own countertransference feelings and to use these to increase their understanding of the analysand's transference and defences'.

The feelings associated with transference are the same for men and women. They include attachment to the analyst, overestimation of the analyst's qualities, and jealousy of those connected with the analyst. Sometimes, transference takes on an exaggerated form known as *acting out*, in which the analysand engages in the impulses stirred up by therapy. However, the analysand must be convinced that 'acting out' the conflict through transference does not constitute a true resolution of the problem. By itself, then, transference does not bring about the required change.

Quite clearly, transference is crucial, because without it the analyst's interpretations would not even be considered by the analysand. Freud believed that psychoanalysis was ineffective with disorders like schizophrenia and depression, because people with these disorders could not produce transference. Whilst he believed that schizophrenia's and depression's origins could be explained in psychodynamic terms, they reduce the capacity for transference for some reason, and since people experiencing those disorders are completely indifferent to the analyst, the analyst cannot influence them.

Achieving insight and working through

Once an analysand consciously understands the roots of the conflict, *insight* has been achieved, and the analysand must be helped to deal with the conflict in a mature and rational way. Whilst insight sometimes comes from the recovery of the memory of a repressed experience, the notion of a psychoanalytic 'cure' resulting from the sudden recall of a single traumatic incident cannot be true, since psychodynamic therapists feel that troubles seldom stem from a single source. Instead, they are *over-determined*. For Freud, analysands gained insight through a gradual increase in self-knowledge (a process of *re-education*). This increase often involves repetitive consideration of all aspects of the conflict, allowing the individual to face reality and deal with it effectively, rather than deny and distort it. This is called *working through*.

To break down the complex ego defences which have been developed to cope with the conflict, and to bring about a lasting personality change, the analysand and analyst need to work through every implication of the problem with complete understanding by the analysand. This is necessary to prevent the conflict from being repressed into the unconscious again. As a result, the individual is strengthened and, therefore, becomes capable of handling different aspects of the conflict without having to resort to *defence mechanisms*. The ultimate goal of psychoanalysis, then, is a deep-seated modification of personality so as to allow people to deal with problems on a realistic basis.

Box 2.5   *Contemporary perspectives on classical psychoanalysis*

Classical psychoanalysis is both intense, time-consuming and expensive (£25 to £35 per 50-minute session), involving perhaps three to six sessions per week over several years. Moreover, during its course, an analysand may be vulnerable and helpless for long periods. This occurs when the analysand's old defences and resistances are broken down, but the ego is still not strong enough to cope adequately with the conflict. Although some psychoanalysts still rigidly adhere to Freud's protracted techniques, there has been a shift in the theoretical basis of psychoanalysis and:

'the Aunt Sally of classical Freudianism is simply not relevant to present-day psychoanalysis' (Holmes, 1996).

For Garfield & Bergin (1994):

'The cornerstones of early Freudian metapsychology were repression, the unconscious, and infantile sexuality. Contemporary psychoanalysis views all three in a different light'.

Psychoanalytically oriented psychotherapies

Analysts who are more flexible in fitting the therapeutic sessions to a person's needs are known as *psychoanalytically oriented psychotherapists*. Most psychoanalytically oriented psychotherapies involve briefer treatment and use face-to-face interaction (*focal psychotherapies*). Although they also emphasise restructuring the entire personality, more attention is paid to the analysand's current life and relationships than to early childhood conflicts. Freudian principles are followed (the aim of therapy is still to gain insight and free expression is emphasised), but these therapies enable those who cannot afford protracted therapy or whose time is limited by other commitments to be treated (Cohn, 1994).

Perhaps the most influential of those who have revised Freudian therapeutic approaches are the *ego psychologists* or *ego analysts*. Rather than emphasising the id's role, these therapists focus on the ego and the way in which it acts as the *executive* (the rational, decision-making part) of personality (see Gross & McIlveen, 1998). As well as personality being shaped by inner conflicts, contemporary analysts believe that it may be shaped by the external environment.

Box 2.6   *Contemporary therapeutic approaches derived from psychoanalysis*

Ego analysts are sometimes referred to as the *second generation* of psychoanalysts. They believe that Freud over-emphasised the influence of sexual and aggressive impulses and underestimated the ego's importance. Erikson, for example, spoke to clients directly about their values and concerns, and encouraged them to consciously fashion particular behaviours and characteristics. For Erikson, the ego's cognitive processes are constructive, creative and productive. This is different from Freud's therapeutic approach of establishing conditions in which patients could 'shore up' the ego's position.

Unlike Freud, who saw analysands as perpetual victims of their past who could not completely overcome their childhood conflicts, Horney saw them as capable of overcoming abuse and deprivation through self-understanding and productive adult relationships. Freud's emphasis on unconscious forces and conflicts was disputed by Anna Freud (Freud's daughter). She believed a better approach was to concentrate on the ways in which the ego perceives the world.

Klein and Mahler have stressed the child's separation from the mother and interpersonal relationships as being important in psychological growth. *Object relations theorists* believe that some people have difficulty in telling where the influences of significant others end and their 'real selves' begin. Mahler's approach to therapy is to help people separate their own ideas and feelings from those of others so they can develop as true individuals.

As noted earlier, one of the major differences between classical psychoanalysis and psychoanalytically oriented psychotherapies is the *time* spent in therapy. Roth & Fonagy (1996) argue that there is a high 'relapse rate' in all types of brief therapies when those who have undergone treatment are not followed up for long periods of time. Therapy's ultimate goal must be good outcome sustained at follow-up, but as Holmes (1996) has remarked:

'Modern health services seem always to be in a hurry; time is money; but the cost of major cardiac surgery is still far greater than, say, the 100–200 hours of psychotherapy that are needed to make a significant impact on borderline personality disorder. An emphasis on sufficient time is a central psychoanalytic dimension that should be preserved at all costs'.

Psychodynamic approaches to group therapy

According to Roberts (1995), the power of the group process for change and healing has been discovered, forgotten and rediscovered on numerous occasions in Britain. One of the earliest uses of *group psychotherapy* was Bion's (1961) attempt to treat neurotic and psychotic soldiers. Since this pioneering work, various group approaches to psychodynamically-oriented therapy have been devised (Brown & Zinkin, 1994). Two of these are *psychodrama* and *transactional analysis*.

Psychodrama

Psychodrama was originated by Moreno (1946), who believed that most human problems arise from the need to maintain social roles which may conflict with each other and a person's essential self. For Moreno, this conflict is the source of a person's anxiety. In the therapy, participants and other group members act out their emotional conflicts. The individual dramatising the conflicts is the *protagonist*, who chooses other group members to represent the conflict's key figures. These *auxiliary egos* are briefed by being given full descriptions of their roles.

Once the protagonist has 'set the scene' by describing it in words and with the aid of very simple props, the interpersonal events are recreated by role play. For example, a male who is terrified of women may be literally 'put on stage' with a female group member who plays his mother. The two are then required to act out a childhood scene with, if necessary, other group members assuming the role of the father, brothers, sisters and so on. The aim is not for dramatic excellence but, in this example, to reveal the sources of the individual's fear of women (Kipper, 1992).

Box 2.7 *Role reversal, doubling and mirroring*

The basic pattern can be varied in several ways. In *role reversal*, the 'actors' switch roles, whilst in *doubling*, the therapist or group leader also acts out the protagonist's role and suggests feelings, motives and so on that might be operating within the protagonist, but which he or she has not yet identified. *Mirroring* involves group members minimising or exaggerating the protagonist's behaviour in order to provide feedback.

Psychodrama's goal is to reveal to the protagonist why he or she is behaving in a particular way. For Moreno, psychodrama is useful because (a) it helps to prevent destructive and irrational acting out in everyday life, (b) it enables feelings which cannot be adequately described or explained to be expressed more fully, and (c) it encourages individuals to reveal the deepest roots of their problems.

Transactional analysis

According to Berne (1964), personality is comprised of *three ego states*, and our behaviour at any given time is determined by one of these states. The *parent* state is that part of personality which stands for the cautions and prohibitions upheld by society and which we learn from our parents. The *child* state is the opposite, and is demanding, dependent and impulsive, seeking gratification of all its wishes *now*. The *adult* state is the mature, rational aspect of personality, which is flexible and adapts to new situations as they arise. Berne did not mean to imply that these three states equate with the id (child), ego (adult) and superego (parent), since the id, ego and superego are, to varying degrees, unconscious. For Berne, we are capable of being fully conscious of the child and parent ego states.

Box 2.8   *Complementary and crossed interactions*

Like Freud, Berne believed that mental disorders occur when one of the ego states comes to dominate the personality. Many interactions between people are *complementary*, that is, aspects of their personalities are matched. For example, the interaction between two people's adult states produces a rational and mature interaction, as when one person says, 'These data don't make any sense' and the other replies, 'I agree. Let's run them through the computer again'. When the aspects of personality operating do not match, the interactions are *crossed*, and this is when problems arise (Baron, 1989). For example, a passenger in a car operating in the child state, might say, 'Come on, let's see if we can get 100 mph out of this car'. The driver, operating in the adult state, might reply, 'No way. If the police are about, we'll be in big trouble'.

Berne argued that crossed interactions often take the form of 'games', interactions which leave both people feeling upset or angry and prevent spontaneous and appropriate behaviour. In *uproar*, one person baits another (Berne, 1976). The other responds in kind, and the exchange escalates until one person storms off in anger. Transactional analysis concentrates on people's tendencies to manipulate others in destructive and non-productive ways. However, unlike psychoanalysis, it focuses on the *present* rather than the past. Through role play, the ego states are identified as they are used in various personal transactions.

This *structural analysis* enables people to understand their behaviour and change it in a way which will give them greater control over their life. Although this is usually initially conducted on an individual basis, the person later participates in group *transactions* (or transactional analysis 'proper'). This involves experimenting, by enacting more appropriate ego states and observing the effects of these on the self and others. By analysing such games, basic conflicts may come to the surface, and these can then be discussed openly, the aim being to show that whilst people's coping patterns may feel natural, they are actually destructive and there are better ways of relating to others.

Therapies based on the psychodynamic model: some issues

At least some people who have undergone psychoanalysis claim that it has helped them achieve insight into their problems, and has provided long-term relief from the repressed feelings that were interfering with healthy functioning. However, although Freud's theories and his therapeutic approach have been influential, they have also been the subject of much criticism, and there have been numerous explanations of 'why Freud was wrong' (Webster, 1995) and several calls to 'bury Freud' (Tallis, 1996). Perhaps the major problem with Freud's work is that it is difficult to study scientifically, since concepts like transference, insight, unconscious conflicts and repression are either vague or difficult to measure.

Evaluating the effectiveness of any therapeutic approach is, as Chapter 6 illustrates, extremely difficult. With psychoanalysis, however, the problems are particularly acute. Much of the evidence favouring psychoanalysis derives from carefully selected case studies, which may be biased. In cases where psychoanalysis fails to produce significant changes, analysts can blame the analysand. If an analysand accepts an insight into a behaviour but does not change that behaviour, the insight is said to be merely *intellectual* (Carlson, 1988).

Box 2.9 *Psychoanalysis as a closed system*

The 'escape clause' of intellectual insight makes the argument for insight's importance completely circular and therefore illogical: if the analysand improves, the improvement is due to insight, but if the analysand's behaviour remains unchanged, then real insight did not occur. Carlson (1988) likens this to the logic of wearing a charm in the belief that it will cure an illness. If the illness is cured, then the charm works. If it is not cured, then the individual does not believe sufficiently in its power. Psychoanalysis is a *closed system*. A critic who raises questions about the validity of psychoanalysis is described as suffering from *resistance*, since the critic cannot recognise the therapy's 'obvious' value.

Conclusions

This chapter has examined psychodynamically-based therapies. Although less popular than they once were, such therapies are still used today. However, several important issues surround their use, and at least some professionals believe them to be of little help in the treatment of mental disorders.

Summary

- The purpose of **psychoanalysis** is to uncover the unconscious conflicts responsible for an individual's mental disorder and make them conscious. By providing **insight** into these, the ego can deal more effectively with them.
- Freud used a variety of techniques to break down an **analysand's** defences, including **hypnosis**, **dream interpretation**, the interpretation of **parapraxes** (**Freudian slips**) and **physiological cues**. However, the most widely used technique is **free association**.

- The **basic rule** of psychoanalysis is that the analysand says whatever comes to mind, since this bypasses the ego's role as a **censor** of threatening unconscious impulses. The analyst acts as a **sounding board**, offering **interpretive comments** and drawing attention to the analysand's **resistances**.

- As therapy progresses, the analyst may **privately deduce** what lies behind the analysand's free associations. Other techniques include **confrontation** and **reconstruction**. When the unconscious conflict has been brought into consciousness, it can be manipulated by the analyst through the **transference/transference neurosis**. Transference may take the form of **acting out**.

- The ultimate goal of psychoanalysis is a deep-seated modification of personality to allow people to deal with problems in a realistic way, without having to resort to **defence mechanisms**. However, **insight** does not constitute a 'cure'. Insight is achieved through a process of 're-education' and increase in self-knowledge involving **working through**.

- **Psychoanalytically oriented psychotherapies** are more flexible and briefer Freudian approaches, and involve face-to-face interaction. Freudian principles are still followed, although more attention is paid to the analysand's current life and relationships.

- Important revisions of Freudian approaches have been made by the **ego psychologists/ego analysts**, who focus on the ego rather than the id. Personality is seen as being shaped as much by the external environment as inner conflicts. This 'second generation' includes Erikson, Horney, Anna Freud, Klein and Mahler.

- Psychodynamic approaches to **group psychotherapy** include Moreno's **psychodrama** and Berne's **transactional analysis**. Psychodrama helps to prevent destructive acting out in everyday life, and encourages individuals to reveal the deepest roots of their problems. Transactional analysis tries to show how 'natural' coping patterns can actually be destructive, and that there are better ways of relating to others.

- Although influential, Freud's theories and his therapeutic approach have been extensively criticised. Much of the evidence for Freud's approach comes from carefully selected case studies. When analysis fails, the analyst can blame the analysand. When an analysand accepts an insight but does not change behaviour, insight is only **intellectual**.
- Critics contend that psychoanalysis is a **closed system**. A critic who raises questions about the validity of psychoanalysis is described as suffering from **resistance**, since he or she cannot recognise the therapy's 'obvious value'.

THERAPIES BASED ON THE BEHAVIOURAL MODEL

3

Introduction and overview

As Chapter 2 showed, psychodynamic therapies' attempts to produce insight into the causes of maladaptive behaviour sometimes result in it being replaced by adaptive behaviour. However, insight often does not result in behavioural change. Also, the majority of psychodynamically-oriented therapies insist on using *childhood* conflicts as a way of explaining present behaviours. According to the behavioural model, it is much better to focus on the behaviour giving rise to a problem rather than the historical reasons for its development.

Therapies based on the behavioural model therefore attempt to change behaviour by whatever means are most effective. The term *behaviour therapy* has been used to describe any therapeutic approach deriving from the behavioural model. However, this does not allow us to determine whether the principles of classical or operant conditioning are being used as the treatment method. Walker (1984) has suggested that the term *behaviour therapy* be confined to those therapies based on *classical conditioning*. Those techniques based on *operant conditioning* are more appropriately described as *behaviour modification techniques*. This chapter considers the application of therapies based on the behavioural model to the treatment of mental disorders.

Therapies based on classical conditioning: behaviour therapy

Watson & Rayner (1920) showed that by repeatedly pairing a neutral stimulus with an unpleasant one, a fear response to the neutral stimulus could be classically conditioned. If maladaptive behaviours can be learned, they can presumably be *unlearned*, since the same principles governing the learning of adaptive behaviours apply to maladaptive ones. Therapies based on classical conditioning concentrate on stimuli that elicit new responses which are contrary to the old, maladaptive ones. Three therapeutic approaches designed to treat phobic behaviour are *implosion therapy*, *flooding* and *systematic desensitisation*. Two therapies designed to treat other disorders (*aversion therapy* and *covert sensitisation*) exert their effects by creating phobias.

Implosion therapy and flooding

Implosion therapy and flooding both work on the principle that if the stimulus evoking a fear response is repeatedly presented without the unpleasant experience that accompanies it, its power to elicit the fear response will be lost.

Implosion therapy

In implosion therapy, the therapist repeatedly exposes the person to vivid mental images of the feared stimulus in the safety of the therapeutic setting. This is achieved by the therapist getting the person to imagine the most terrifying form of contact with the feared object using *stimulus augmentation* (vivid verbal descriptions of the feared stimulus, to supplement the person's imagery). After repeated trials, the stimulus eventually loses its anxiety-producing power and the anxiety extinguishes (or *implodes*), because no harm comes to the individual in the safe setting of the therapist's room.

Flooding

In flooding, the individual is forced to *confront* the object or situation eliciting the fear response. For example, a person with a fear of heights might be taken to the top of a tall building and physically prevented from leaving. By preventing avoidance of, or escape from, the feared object or situation, the fear response is eventually extinguished. Wolpe (1973) describes a case in which an adolescent girl afraid of cars was forced into the back of one. She was then driven around continuously for four hours. Initially, her fear reached hysterical heights. Eventually, it receded, and by the end of the journey had disappeared completely.

Implosion therapy and flooding are effective with certain types of phobia (Emmelkamp *et al.*, 1992). However, for some people, both lead to increased anxiety, and the procedures are too traumatic. As a result, they are used with considerable caution.

Box 3.1   *Using virtual reality to treat phobias*

Computer-generated virtual environments have been tested on people suffering from various phobias. The hardware consists of a head-mounted display and a sensor that tracks head and right hand movements so that the user can interact with objects in the virtual environment. The equipment is integrated with a square platform surrounded by a railing. This aids exposure by giving the user something to hold on to and an edge to feel.

Figure 3.1   *Head-mounted display, similar to that used in the treatment of people with phobias*

Software creates a number of virtual environments to confront different phobias. Those for acrophobia include:

- three footbridges hovering 7, 50 and 80 metres above water;
- four outdoor balconies with railings at various heights in a building ranging up to 20 floors high;
- a glass elevator simulating the one at Atlanta's Marriott Hotel which rises 49 floors.

People using virtual reality:

'had the same sensations and anxiety as they did in vivo. They were sweating, weak at the knees and had butterflies in the stomach. When the elevator went up and down, they really felt it. We are trying to help people confront what they are scared of' (Rothbaum, cited in Dobson, 1996).

Rothbaum sees virtual reality as holding the key to the treatment of phobia because it is easier to arrange and less traumatic than real exposure to phobia-causing situations. Compared with a control group of acrophobics, Rothbaum and her team reported a 100 per cent improvement in 12 participants after two months of 'treatment'.

Systematic desensitisation

Implosion therapy and flooding both use extinction to alter behaviour. However, neither trains people to substitute the maladaptive behaviour (such as fear) with an adaptive and *desirable* response. Jones (1924) showed that fear responses could be eliminated if children were given candy and other incentives in the presence of the feared object. Her method involved *gradually* introducing the feared object, bringing it closer and closer to the children whilst at the same time giving them candy, until no anxiety was elicited in its presence. For many years, Jones's work went unrecognised. Wolpe (1958) popularised and refined it under the name *systematic desensitisation* (SD).

The therapy requires that an individual initially constructs an *anxiety hierarchy* (a series of scenes or events rated from lowest to highest in terms of the amount of anxiety they elicit: see Box 3.2, page 39).

Once the hierarchy has been constructed, *relaxation training* is given. This will be the adaptive substitute response and is the response most therapists use. Training aims to achieve complete relaxation, the essential task being to respond quickly to suggestions to feel relaxed and peaceful. After relaxation training, the person is asked to imagine, as vividly as possible, the scene at the bottom of the hierarchy, and is simultaneously told to remain calm and relaxed.

Box 3.2 *An anxiety hierarchy generated by a person with thanatophobia (where 1 = no anxiety and 100 = extreme anxiety)*

Ratings	Items
5	Seeing an ambulance
10	Seeing a hospital
20	Being inside a hospital
25	Reading an obituary notice of an old person
30–40	Passing a funeral home
40–55	Seeing a funeral
55–65	Driving past a cemetery
70	Reading the obituary of a young person who died of a heart attack
80	Seeing a burial assemblage from a distance
90	Being at a funeral
100	Seeing a dead man in a coffin

(Based on Wolpe & Wolpe, 1981)

Box 3.3 *Reciprocal inhibition and SD*

Wolpe was influenced by the concept of *reciprocal inhibition* which, as applied to phobias, maintains that it is impossible to experience two incompatible emotional states (such as anxiety and relaxation) at the same time. If the individual finds that anxiety is *increasing*, the image is terminated, and the therapist attempts to help him or her regain the sense of relaxation. When thinking about the scene at the hierarchy's bottom no longer elicits anxiety, the next scene in the hierarchy is presented. *Systematically*, the hierarchy is worked through until the individual can imagine any of the scenes without experiencing discomfort. When this happens, the person is *desensitised*. Once the hierarchy has been worked through, the person is required to confront the anxiety-producing stimulus in the real world.

One problem with SD is its dependence on a person's ability to conjure up vivid images of encounters with a phobic object or situation. A way of overcoming this is to use photographs or slides displaying the feared object or situation. Another approach involves live (*in vivo*) encounters. For example, an arachnophobic may be desensitised by gradually approaching spiders, the method used by Jones (see above). *In vivo* desensitisation is almost always more effective and longer lasting than other desensitisation techniques (Wilson & O'Leary, 1978).

SD, implosion therapy and flooding are all effective in dealing with specific fears and anxieties. Compared with one another, flooding is more effective than SD (Marks, 1987) and implosion therapy (Emmelkamp *et al.*, 1992), whilst implosion therapy and SD do not differ in their effectiveness (Gelder *et al.*, 1989).

The fact that flooding is apparently the superior therapy suggests that *in vivo* exposure to the anxiety's source is crucial. Because implosion therapy and SD do not differ in their effectiveness, systematically working through a hierarchy might not be necessary. Indeed, presenting the hierarchy in reverse order (from most to least frightening), randomly, or in the standard way (from least to most frightening) does not influence SD's effectiveness (Marks, 1987).

Aversion therapy

The therapies just considered are all appropriate in the treatment of phobias occurring in specific situations. Aversion therapy, by contrast, is used with people who want to *extinguish* the *pleasant* feelings associated with socially undesirable behaviours, like excessive drinking or smoking. SD tries to substitute a pleasurable response for an aversive one. Aversion therapy *reverses* this and pairs an unpleasant event with a desired but socially undesirable behaviour. If this unpleasant event and desired behaviour are repeatedly paired, the desired behaviour should eventually elicit negative responses.

Box 3.4 *Aversion therapy and alcohol abuse*

Perhaps aversion therapy's most well-known application has been in the treatment of alcohol abuse. In one method, the problem drinker is given a drug that induces nausea and vomiting, but *only* when combined with alcohol. When a drink is taken, the alcohol interacts with the drug to produce nausea and vomiting. It does not take many pairings before alcohol begins to elicit an aversive fear response (becoming nauseous).

In another method, the problem drinker is given a warm saline solution containing a drug which induces nausea and vomiting without alcohol. Immediately before vomiting begins, an alcoholic beverage is given, and the person is required to smell, taste and swill it around the mouth before swallowing it. The aversive fear response may *generalise* to other alcohol-related stimuli, such as pictures of bottles containing alcohol. However, to avoid generalisation to all drinks, the individual may be required to take a soft drink in between the aversive conditioning trials.

Aversion therapy has been used with some success in the treatment of alcohol abuse and other behaviours (most notably cigarette smoking, overeating and children's self-injurious behaviour). It has also found its way into popular culture. In Burgess's (1962) novel *A Clockwork Orange*, the anti-social 'hero', Alex, gains great enjoyment from rape and violent behaviour. When caught, he can choose between prison and therapy and opts for the latter. He is given a nausea-inducing drug and required to watch films of violence and rape. After his release, he feels nauseous whenever he contemplates violence and rape. However, because the therapy took place with Beethoven's music playing, Alex acquires an aversion towards Beethoven as well!

One of the most controversial (and non-fictional) applications of aversion therapy has been with sexual 'aberrations' such as homosexuality (Beresford, 1997). Male homosexuals, for example, are shown slides of nude males followed by painful but safe electric shocks. The conditioned response to the slides is intended to generalise to homosexual fantasies and activities beyond the therapeutic setting. Later, the individual may be shown slides of nude women and an electric shock terminated when a sexual response occurs (Adams *et al.*, 1981).

Whatever its use, aversion therapy is unpleasant, and not appropriate without an individual's *consent* or unless all other approaches to treatment have failed. As noted, evidence suggests that the therapy is effective. However, those undergoing it often find ways to continue with their problem behaviours. People have the cognitive abilities to discriminate between the situation in which aversive conditions occur and situations in the real world. In some cases, then, cognitive factors will 'swamp' the conditioning process, and this is one reason why aversion therapy is not always effective.

Aversion therapy does not involve classical conditioning alone and actually combines it with operant conditioning. Once the classically conditioned fear has been established, the person is inclined to avoid future contact with the problem stimulus (an *operant* response), in order to alleviate fear of it (which is *negatively reinforcing*). Critics see aversion therapy as being inappropriate unless the individual learns an *adaptive* response. For this reason, most behaviour therapists try to *shape* (see page 46) new adaptive behaviours at the same time as extinguishing existing maladaptive ones.

Covert sensitisation

Silverstein (1972) has argued that aversion therapy is unethical and has the potential for misuse and abuse. As a response to this, some therapists use covert sensitisation (CS) as an alternative and 'milder' form of aversion therapy. CS is a mixture of aversion therapy and SD. Essentially, people are trained to punish themselves using their *imaginations* (hence the term *covert*). *Sensitisation* is achieved by associating the undesirable behaviour with an exceedingly disagreeable consequence.

Box 3.5 *CS and alcohol abuse*

A heavy drinker might be asked to imagine being violently sick all over him- or herself on entering a bar, and feeling better only after leaving and breathing fresh air. The individual is also instructed to rehearse an alternative 'relief' scene, in which the decision not to drink is accompanied by pleasurable sensations. CS can be helpful in controlling overeating and cigarette smoking as well as excessive drinking (Cautela, 1967).

Therapies based on operant conditioning: behaviour modification techniques

Behaviours under voluntary control are strongly influenced by their consequences. Actions producing positive outcomes tend to be repeated, whereas those producing negative outcomes tend to be suppressed. Therapies based on classical conditioning usually involve *emotional responses* (such as anxiety), although *observable behaviours* (such as gradually approaching an object that elicits anxiety) are also influenced. Therapies based on operant conditioning are aimed *directly* at observable behaviours.

There are several therapies based on operant conditioning, all involving three main steps. The first is to identify the undesirable or maladaptive behaviour. The next is to identify the reinforcers that maintain such behaviour. The final step is to restructure the environment so that the maladaptive behaviour is no longer reinforced. One way to eliminate undesirable behaviours is to remove the reinforcers that maintain them, the idea being that their removal will *extinguish* the behaviour they reinforce. Another way is to use aversive stimuli to punish voluntary maladaptive behaviours.

As well as eliminating undesirable behaviours, operant conditioning can be used to increase desirable behaviours. This can be achieved by providing *positive reinforcement* when a behaviour is performed, and making the reinforcement *contingent* on the behaviour being manifested voluntarily.

Therapies based on extinction

The behavioural model proposes that people learn to behave in abnormal ways when they are unintentionally reinforced by others for doing so. For example, a child who receives parental attention when he or she shouts is likely to engage in this behaviour in the future, because attention is reinforcing. If abnormal behaviours can be *acquired* through operant conditioning, they can be *eliminated* through it. With a disruptive child, parents might be instructed to ignore the behaviour so that it is extinguished from the child's behavioural repertoire.

If this is to be effective, however, the therapist must be able to identify and eliminate the reinforcer that is maintaining the adaptive behaviour, and this is not always easy (Crooks & Stein, 1991).

Box 3.6 *Behaviour modification using extinction*

A 20-year-old woman reluctantly sought help for 'compulsive face-picking'. Whenever the woman found some little blemish or pimple, she would pick and scratch at it until it became a bleeding sore. As a result, her face was unsightly. Everyone was distressed except the individual herself, who seemed remarkably unconcerned. Her family and fiancé had tried several tactics to stop the face-picking, including appealing to her vanity, pleading and making threats.

The therapist felt that the face-picking was being maintained by the attention her family and fiancé were giving it. As long as she continued, the pattern of inadvertent reinforcement was maintained, and she would remain the centre of attention. Once the therapist had identified the behaviours that were reinforcing the face-picking, the parents and fiancé were instructed not to engage in these and to ignore the face-picking entirely. They were also told that it would probably get worse before it improved.

After a temporary increase in face-picking, it was quickly extinguished when attention was no longer given. To prevent the behaviour from reappearing, the parents and fiancé were encouraged to provide plenty of loving attention and to support the woman contingent upon a variety of healthy, adaptive behaviours. (Based on Crooks & Stein, 1991)

Therapies based on punishment

In aversion therapy, an aversive stimulus, such as an electric shock, is used to classically condition a negative response to a desired but undesirable stimulus. Aversive stimuli can also be used to punish voluntary maladaptive behaviours. Cowart & Whaley (1971) studied an emotionally disturbed infant who was hospitalised because he persistently engaged in self-mutilating behaviour to such an extent that he had to be restrained in his crib. Electrodes were attached to the infant's leg, and he was placed in a room with a padded floor (the self-mutilation involved violently banging his head against the floor). When the infant began the self-mutilating behaviour, he was given an electric shock. Initially, he was startled, but continued self-mutilating, at which point another shock was given. There were very few repetitions before self-mutilation stopped, and the infant could be safely let out of his crib.

Box 3.7   *Punishment: effectiveness and ethics*

It is generally agreed that therapies using punishment are not as effective as those employing positive reinforcement (see below) in bringing about behaviour change. At least one reason for not using punishment is the tendency for people to *overgeneralise* behaviour. Thus, behaviours which are *related* to the punished behaviour are also not performed. Moreover, punishment tends to produce only a temporary suppression of undesirable behaviour, and unless another reinforcement-inducing behaviour pattern is substituted for the punished behaviour, it will resurface.

There are also ethical issues surrounding punishment's use, particularly with very young children. In Cowart and Whaley's study, however, the infant was engaging in a behaviour which was clearly very harmful, and with these sorts of behaviour, punishment is actually extremely effective. Presumably, the physical well-being that occurred from not self-mutilating was sufficiently reinforcing to maintain the new behaviour pattern.

Therapies based on positive reinforcement
Behaviour shaping

Isaacs *et al.* (1960) describe the case of a 40-year-old male schizophrenic who had not spoken to anyone for 19 years. Quite accidentally, a therapist discovered that the man loved chewing gum, and decided to use this as a way of getting him to speak.

Initially, the therapist held up a piece of gum. When the patient looked at it, it was given to him. The patient began to pay attention to the therapist and would look at the gum as soon as the therapist removed it from his pocket. Later, the therapist held up the gum and waited until the patient moved his lips. When this occurred, he was immediately given the gum. However, the therapist then began to give the gum *only* when the patient made a sound.

At the point when the patient reliably made a sound when the gum was shown, the therapist held the gum and instructed him to 'Say gum'. After 19 years of silence, the patient said the word. After six weeks, he spontaneously said 'Gum, please', and shortly afterwards began talking to the therapist. This approach is known as *behaviour shaping* and has been most notably used with the chronically disturbed and people with learning difficulties, who are extremely difficult to communicate with.

Box 3.8 *Using positive reinforcement to treat anorexia nervosa*

A young anorectic woman was in danger of dying because she had drastically curtailed her eating behaviour and weighed only 47 lbs. In the first stage of therapy, the therapist established an appropriate reinforcer that could be made contingent upon eating. The reinforcer chosen was social, and whenever the anorectic swallowed a bite of food, she was rewarded by the therapist talking to her and paying her attention. If she refused to eat, the therapist left the room and she remained alone until the next meal was served (which is 'time out' from positive reinforcement rather than punishment).

After a while, her eating behaviour gradually increased, and the therapist introduced other rewards contingent upon her continuing

to eat and gain weight. These included having other people join her at meal times or being allowed to have her hair done. Eventually, the woman gained sufficient weight to be discharged from the hospital. Because people are likely to regress if returned to a non-supportive institutional setting, the woman's parents were instructed in ways to continue reinforcing her for appropriate eating behaviours. At follow-up nearly three years later, the woman was still maintaining an adequate weight.
(Based on Bachrach *et al.*, 1965)

Token economies

Ayllon & Haughton (1962) reported that staff at one hospital found it particularly difficult to get withdrawn schizophrenics to eat regularly. Ayllon and Haughton noticed that the staff were actually exacerbating the problem by coaxing the patients into the dining room and, in some cases, even feeding them. The researchers reasoned that the increased attention was reinforcing the patients' uncooperativeness and decided that the hospital rules should be changed. For example, if patients did not arrive at the dining hall within 30 minutes of being called, they were locked out. Additionally, staff were no longer permitted to interact with patients at meal times. Because their uncooperative behaviours were no longer being reinforced, the patients quickly changed their eating habits. Then, the patients were made to pay one penny in order to enter the dining hall. The pennies could be earned by showing socially appropriate *target behaviours*, and their frequency also began to increase.

Ayllon and Haughton's approach was refined by Ayllon & Azrin (1968) in the form of a *token economy system*. In this, disturbed individuals are given tokens in exchange for desirable behaviour. The therapist first identifies what patients like (such as watching television or smoking cigarettes). When a productive activity occurs (such as making a bed or socialising with other patients), a patient is given tokens that can be exchanged for 'privileges'. The tokens therefore become conditioned reinforcers for desirable and appropriate behaviours.

Ayllon and Azrin showed that tokens were effective in eliciting and maintaining desired behaviours. The amount of time spent performing desired behaviours was highest when the reinforcement contingencies were imposed and lowest when they were not. Ayllon and Azrin also discovered that token economies had an effect on patient and staff morale, in that the patients were less apathetic and irresponsible, whilst the staff became more enthusiastic about their patients and the therapeutic techniques.

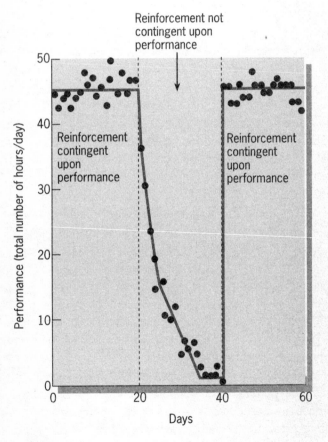

Figure 3.2 *The effects of a token economy on hospitalised patients' performances of target behaviours*

As well as being used with the chronically disturbed, token economies have also been used in programmes designed to modify the behaviour of children with *conduct disorders*. Schneider & Byrne (1987) awarded tokens to children who engaged in helpful behaviours and removed the tokens for inappropriate behaviours, such as arguing or not paying attention.

Box 3.9 *Token economies: some issues*

Despite their effectiveness in producing behaviour change with various disorders, issues have been raised about token economies. Eventually, tokens will have to be replaced by other social reinforcers, both within and outside the therapeutic setting. The individual is gradually 'weaned off' the tokens in the therapeutic setting, and can be transferred to a 'half-way house' or some other community live-in arrangement where more social reinforcers can be used. Unfortunately, this is not always successful, and there tends to be a high re-hospitalisation rate for discharged individuals.

Token economies can lead to 'token learning' (people might only indulge in a behaviour if they are directly rewarded for it: Baddeley, 1997). Whilst this might be effective within the confines of the therapeutic setting, Baddeley sees it as quite unproductive in other settings, where it is necessary to learn on a subtler and less immediate reward system.

Some general comments about therapies based on the behavioural model

One criticism of therapies based on the behavioural model is that they focus only on the observable aspects of a disorder. The behavioural model considers the maladaptive behaviour to be the disorder, and the disorder is 'cured' when the behaviour is changed. Although critics accept that therapies based on the behavioural model can alter behaviour, they argue that such therapies fail to identify a disorder's *underlying* causes. One consequence of this is *symptom substitution*, in which removing one symptom simply results in another, and perhaps one more serious, occurring in some other form.

As noted earlier, behaviours learnt under one set of conditions may not generalise to other conditions. The behavioural model sees behaviours as being controlled by the environment, so it is not surprising that behaviours altered in one context do not endure in a very different one. Indeed, Rimm (1976) sees this as behaviour therapy's major limitation. To avoid this, therapists attempt to extend the generality of changed behaviours by working (as far as possible) in environments which are representative of real life. They also encourage people to avoid environments that elicit maladaptive behaviours, to return for follow-up treatment, and teach them how to modify their behaviour on a continuing basis.

The most serious criticism of behaviour therapy and modification is ethical. Techniques involving punishment, in particular, have been criticised for exercising authoritarian control and for dehumanising and 'brainwashing' people. Another criticism is that behaviour therapists manipulate people and deprive them of their freedom. As has been seen, it is the therapist, rather than the person, who controls the reinforcers, and therapists do not encourage people to seek insight concerning their disorders.

However, supporters of the behavioural model argue that they do not treat disorders without consent and that, in a sense, we are all 'naïve behaviour therapists'. For example, when we praise people or tell them off for a particular behaviour, we are using behaviour modification techniques: all therapists are doing is using such approaches in a systematic and consistent way. Therapists who use behavioural methods are not attempting to control behaviour, but helping people to control their *own* behaviours.

Conclusions

Various behaviour therapies and behaviour modification techniques have been used to treat mental disorders. Although supporters of the behavioural model see the therapies as being highly effective, opponents believe that important criticisms can be made of them which limit their application.

Summary

- Therapies based on the behavioural model try to change behaviour based on whatever means are most effective. **Behaviour therapies** use classical conditioning principles whilst **behaviour modification techniques** use operant conditioning.

- If maladaptive behaviours can be learned through classical conditioning, they can presumably be unlearned by the same principles. **Implosion therapy**, **flooding**, and **systematic desensitisation** (SD) are used to treat phobias, and attempt to produce new responses that are contrary to the old, maladaptive ones.

- Neither implosion therapy nor flooding trains people to substitute maladaptive behaviour with adaptive/desirable behaviour. SD does, with **relaxation** being the adaptive substitute response used by most therapists.

- Flooding is more effective than SD and implosion therapy. Implosion therapy and SD are equally effective. This suggests that **in vivo** exposure to the phobic stimulus is important, and that systematic progression through a hierarchy is unnecessary.

- **Aversion therapy** is used to extinguish the pleasant feelings associated with an undesirable behaviour. This is achieved by repeatedly pairing an unpleasant stimulus with the undesirable behaviour until it eventually elicits an unpleasant response. This therapy uses both classical and operant conditioning.

- Although useful in the treatment of some problem behaviours, there are important ethical issues associated with aversion therapy's use. For that reason, **covert sensitisation** is sometimes employed. This method has been used to control excessive drinking, overeating and smoking.

- Behaviour therapies usually involve emotional responses as well as observable behaviours. Therapies based on operant conditioning are aimed **directly** at observable behaviours. When the reinforcers that maintain an undesirable/maladaptive behaviour have been identified, the environment is restructured so that they are no longer reinforced.

- Undesirable behaviours can be **extinguished** by removing the reinforcers that maintain them. Alternatively, aversive stimuli can be used to **punish** the behaviours. Desirable behaviours can be increased by making **positive reinforcement** contingent on voluntary behaviours being performed.

- **Punishment** by electric shock has been used to treat self-mutilating behaviour. However, punishment only suppresses an undesirable behaviour, which will resurface unless substituted by a behaviour that is reinforced. Punishment also raises ethical issues, particularly when used to treat children.

- **Behaviour shaping** and the **token economy** system both use **positive reinforcement** to change behaviour. These methods are effective in eliciting and maintaining desired behaviours. However, they are limited by a lack of generalisation beyond the therapeutic setting. Token economies, for example, can lead to 'token learning'. To avoid lack of generalisation, therapists try to work in environments that are as representative of real life as possible.

- By focusing on a disorder's observable aspects, therapies based on the behavioural model fail to identify its underlying causes. One consequence of this is **symptom substitution**. Although critics accept that such therapies can be effective, they see therapists as manipulating, dehumanising, and controlling people and depriving them of their freedom. Therapists sees themselves helping people to control their own behaviour.

THERAPIES BASED ON THE COGNITIVE MODEL

Introduction and overview

The cognitive model sees mental disorders as resulting from distortions in people's cognitions. The aim of cognitively based therapies is to show people that their distorted or irrational thoughts are the main contributors to their difficulties. If faulty modes of thinking can be *modified* or *changed*, then disorders can be alleviated.

Therapies based on the cognitive model, then, have the goal of changing maladaptive behaviour by changing the way people think. Cognitive therapies have been viewed as a collection of techniques really belonging to the domain of the behavioural model (and thus the term *cognitive–behavioural therapies* is sometimes used to describe them). In some cases, the dividing line between a therapy based on the behavioural model and one based on the cognitive model is very fine and arbitrary. Indeed, therapists identifying their orientation as primarily behavioural or cognitive may actually be doing the same thing.

Supporters of the cognitive model, however, believe that behaviour change results from changes in cognitive processes, and hence cognitively based therapies can be separated from behavioural ones. Like psychodynamic therapies, cognitive therapies aim to produce insight. However, rather than focusing on the past, they try to produce insight into *current cognitions*. This chapter begins by looking at therapeutic approaches devised by Bandura who, whilst often considered a behaviour therapist, attempts to change behaviour by altering thoughts and perceptions. It continues with an examination of Ellis' *rational–emotive therapy*, Beck's *cognitive therapy for depression*, *attributional therapy*, Meichenbaum's *stress inoculation therapy*, and some more recent cognitively based applications.

Bandura's approaches to therapy

Many behavioural therapists incorporate cognitive processes into their theoretical outlook and cognitive procedures into their methodology (Wilson, 1982). Techniques like SD and covert sensitisation, for example, use *visual imagery*. The interface between behavioural methods and the cognitive model is called *cognitive–behavioural therapy*, and a leading researcher is Bandura.

Certain kinds of learning cannot be *solely* explained in terms of classical or operant conditioning. According to Bandura (1969) and other *social learning theorists*, humans and some non-humans can learn directly *without* experiencing an event, and can acquire new forms of behaviour from others simply by observing them (*observational learning*). Moreover, whether we see people being rewarded or punished can strengthen or reduce our own inhibitions against behaving in similar ways. If we see a positive outcome for a behaviour, our restraint against performing it is lowered (*response disinhibition*). However, if we see a negative outcome, our restraint is heightened (*response inhibition*).

Bandura argues that maladaptive behaviours can be altered by exposing those demonstrating them to appropriate *models* (others performing actions the person is afraid to perform). As well as changing behaviour, this approach aims to change thoughts and perceptions.

Box 4.1 illustrates *participant modelling,* which involves the individual observing the therapist's behaviour and then imitating it. This method is more effective than having people watch filmed or video-taped models (*symbolic modelling*). Modelling has been successfully used with a variety of phobias and, as well as eliminating undesirable behaviours, has also been used to establish new and more appropriate behaviours.

Box 4.1 *An application of modelling*

The therapist performed the behaviour fearlessly at each step and gradually led participants into touching, stroking and then holding the snake's body with gloved and bare hands, whilst the experimenter held the snake securely by the head and tail. If a participant was unable to touch the snake following ample demonstration, she was asked to place her hands on the experimenter's and to move her hand down gradually until it touched the snake's body. After the participants no longer felt any apprehension about touching the snake under these conditions, anxieties about contact with the snake's head area and entwining tail were extinguished.

The therapist again performed the tasks fearlessly, and then the experimenter and the participant performed the responses jointly. As participants became less fearful, the experimenter gradually reduced his participation and control over the snake, until eventually participants were able to hold the snake in their laps without assistance, to let the snake loose in the room and retrieve it, and to let it crawl freely over their bodies. Progress through the graded approach tasks was paced according to the participants' apprehensiveness. When they reported being able to perform one activity with little or no fear, they were eased into a more difficult interaction.

(From Bandura, 1971)

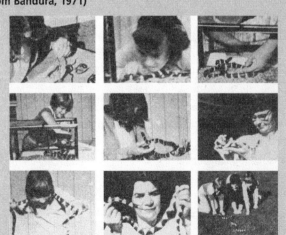

Figure 4.1 *As this sequence of photographs shows, modelling can be an effective way of treating phobias*

In *assertiveness training*, people with difficulty in asserting themselves in interpersonal situations are required to perform in the presence of a group who provide feedback about the adequacy of performance. Then, the therapist assumes the individual's role and models the appropriate assertive behaviour. The individual is asked to try again, this time imitating the therapist. The alternation between *behavioural rehearsal* and modelling continues until the assertive role has been mastered. When this occurs, the skills are tried out in real-life situations. This approach has also been widely used in *social skills training*, in which people who lack the ability to function effectively in certain situations observe others performing the desired behaviours and then attempt to imitate them.

Bandura (1977) believes that one reason for modelling's effectiveness is the development of *self-efficacy*. Being able to perform a behaviour that was previously impossible raises a person's evaluation of the degree to which he or she can cope with difficult situations. According to Bandura, when people encounter new situations in which they have difficulty, they are much more willing to engage in behaviours that were previously avoided.

Ellis' rational–emotive therapy (RET)

Rational–emotive therapy (RET) was developed in the 1950s by Ellis. After becoming dissatisfied with what he called the 'passivity of psychoanalysis', Ellis, a trained psychoanalyst, developed his own therapeutic approach. For several years, this therapy was regarded as being on the periphery. However, RET is now practised by a large number of therapists, particularly in the USA.

Box 4.2 *The A–B–C model*

Ellis (1958, 1962) argues that many emotional difficulties are due to the *irrational beliefs* people bring to bear on their experiences and the reinforcement these receive through being repeated. For Ellis (1991), irrational beliefs can be understood as part of the *A–B–C*

---

model. According to this, a significant activating event (A) is followed by a highly charged emotional consequence (C). However, to say that A is the cause of C is not *always* correct, even though it may appear to be as far as a person is concerned. Rather, Ellis sees C occurring because of a person's belief system (B). Inappropriate emotions, such as depression and guilt, can only be abolished if a change occurs in beliefs and perceptions.

To illustrate this, suppose someone telephones several friends to invite them out for a drink, but finds that none is able to accept the invitation. This activating event (A) might produce the emotional consequence (C) that the person feels depressed, isolated and worthless. For Ellis, C occurs because of the person's belief system (B), which holds that because no one has accepted the invitation, it must mean that no one likes him or her.

The aim of RET is to help people find flaws in their thinking and 'to make mincemeat' of these maladaptive cognitions by creating D, a *dispute belief system* which has no severe emotional consequences. In the example used above, D might run along the lines of 'people have already made plans to go out and just because they can't accept my invitation doesn't mean they don't like me'.

Ellis proposes that two of the most common maladaptive cognitions people hold are (1) they are worthless unless they are perfectly competent at everything they try, and (2) they must be approved of and loved by everyone they meet. Because such beliefs make impossible demands on people who hold them, they lead to anxiety, failure and, frequently, abnormal behaviour.

Box 4.3 *Some common irrational beliefs encountered in RET*

- Certain people I must deal with are thoroughly bad and should be severely blamed and punished for it.
- It is awful and upsetting when things are not the way I would like them to be.
- My unhappiness is always caused by external events; I cannot control my emotional reactions.

- If something unpleasant might happen, I should keep dwelling on it.
- It is easier to avoid difficulties and responsibilities than to face them.
- I should depend on others who are stronger than I am.
- Because something once strongly affected my life, it will do so indefinitely.
- There is always a perfect solution to human problems, and it is awful if this solution is not found.

(Based on Rohsenow & Smith, 1982)

Once the irrational beliefs have been identified, therapy continues by guiding the person to substitute more logical or realistic thoughts for the maladaptive ones, a task which Ellis believes can be accomplished 'by any therapist worth his or her salt'. Ellis sees the rational–emotive therapist as an *exposing and nonsense-annihilating scientist*. Therapists claim that the universe is logical and rational, and the appropriate means of understanding it is the scientific method of controlled observation. People have the *capacity* for rational understanding and the *resources* for personal growth. However, they also have the capacity to delude themselves and accept irrational beliefs.

As noted earlier, the first stage in therapy is for people to recognise and question their irrational beliefs. Rather than remaining 'anonymous', as a classical psychoanalyst would do, and occasionally offering some form of interpretation, the rational–emotive therapist will show the person how to ask questions like '*Where* is the evidence that I am a worthless person if I am not universally approved?', '*Who* says I must be perfect?' and '*Why* must things go exactly the way I would like them to go?'

Once people have recognised and analysed their beliefs, they are taught to substitute more realistic alternatives to engender *full acceptance*. Rather than measuring themselves against impossible standards, a rational–emotive therapist emphasises that failures should not be seen as 'disastrous', confirming a lack of self-worth, but merely as 'unfortunate' events.

> **Box 4.4** *Some rational alternatives to irrational beliefs*
>
> **Irrational belief:** I *must* prove myself to be thoroughly competent, adequate and achieving, or I must at least have real competence or talent at something important.
> **Rational alternative belief:** What I do doesn't have to be perfect to be good. I will be happier if I achieve at a realistic level rather than strive for perfection.
> **Irrational belief:** I *have* to view life as awful, terrible, horrible, or catastrophic when things do not go the way I would like them to go.
> **Rational alternative belief:** If I can't change the situation, it may be unfortunate but not catastrophic. I can make plans for my life to be as enjoyable as possible.
> **Irrational belief:** I *must* have sincere love and approval almost all the time from all the people who are significant to me.
> **Rational alternative belief:** I would *like* to be approved, but I do not *need* such approval.
> (Based on Lange & Jakubowksi, 1976)

Rational–emotive therapists use various approaches to minimise self-defeating beliefs. Rather than focusing on people's histories, they focus on the 'here and now'. As Ellis (1984) has put it:

> 'Therapists do not spend a great deal of time ... encouraging long tales of woe, sympathetically getting in tune with emotionalising or carefully and incisively reflecting feelings.'

Ellis is not interested in what he calls 'long-winded dialogues', which he sees as 'indulgent'. Rather, RET aims to help people *get* better rather than *feel* better during a therapy session, and to accept reality 'even when it is pretty grim'.

Indeed, by providing people with warmth, support, attention and caring, their need for love (which is usually the central core of their circumstances: Elkins, 1980) is reinforced. There is also the possibility that people become dependent on the therapy and the therapist. The direct approach used in RET is illustrated in Box 4.5, in which Ellis discusses the problems experienced by a 25-year-old female.

Box 4.5 *RET in action*

Therapist: The same crap! It's always the same crap. Now, if you would look at the crap – instead of 'Oh, how stupid I am! He hates me! I think I'll kill myself!' – then you'd get better right away.

Person: You've been listening! (*laughs*)

Therapist: Listening to what?

Person: (*laughs*) Those wild statements in my mind, like that, that I make.

Therapist: That's right! Because I know that you have to make those statements – because I have a good theory. And according to my theory, people couldn't get upset unless they made those nutty statements to themselves ... Even if I loved you madly, the next person you talk to is likely to hate you. So I like brown eyes and he likes blue eyes, or something. So then you're dead! Because you really think: 'I've got to be accepted! I've got to act intelligently!' Well, why?

Person: (*very soberly and reflectively*) True.

Therapist: You see?

Person: Yes.

Therapist: Now, if you will learn that lesson, then you've had a very valuable session. Because you don't have to upset yourself. As I said before: if I thought you were the worst [*expletive deleted*] who ever existed, well that's my opinion. And I'm entitled to it. But does that make you a turd?

Person: (*reflective silence*)

Therapist: Does it?

Person: No.

Therapist: What makes you a turd?

Person: *Thinking* that you are.

Therapist: That's right! Your *belief* that you are. That's the only thing that could ever do it. And you never have to believe that. See? You control your thinking. I control my thinking – *my* belief about you. But you don't have to be affected by that. You *always* control what you think.

(From Ellis, 1984)

RET seems to be effective for at least some types of disorder (Emmelkamp *et al.*, 1978). However, for other disorders (such as agoraphobia) RET is less effective than therapies derived from other models (Haaga & Davison, 1993). Clearly, RET is an active and directive therapeutic approach, and one in which the therapist's personal beliefs and values are an inevitable part of what goes on during therapy. However, Ellis' (1984) views that 'no one and nothing is supreme', that 'self-gratification' should be encouraged and that 'unequivocal love, commitment, service and … fidelity to any interpersonal commitment, especially marriage, leads to harmful consequences' have been disputed (e.g. Bergin, 1980).

The argumentative approach to therapy, in which the therapist attacks those beliefs regarded as foolish and illogical, has also been questioned, particularly by those who stress the importance of *empathy* in therapy (see Chapter 5). For example, Fancher (1995) believes that all cognitive therapies rely on a common-sense view of cognition, and falsely assume that therapists are capable of identifying 'faulty thinking': what is foolish and illogical to the therapist may not be foolish and illogical in terms of the individual's own experiences.

RET is effective in producing behaviour change amongst those who are self-demanding and feel guilty for not living up to their own standards of perfection (Brandsma *et al.*, 1978). For people with severe thought disorders (as in schizophrenia), however, the therapy is ineffective, since people with such disorders do not respond to an Ellis-type analysis of their problems (Ellis, 1993).

Beck's cognitive restructuring therapy

Like Ellis, Beck (1967) was originally trained as a psychoanalyst. As with RET, Beck's therapy assumes that disorders stem primarily from irrational beliefs that cause people to behave in maladaptive ways. Beck's approach is specifically designed to treat *depressed* people. Depressed people suffer from a *cognitive triad* of negative beliefs about themselves, their futures and their experiences (Beck *et al.*, 1979). Such beliefs are seen as arising from faulty information-processing and faulty logic.

Several types of faulty thinking can contribute to depression (see Gross & McIlveen, 1998). As noted, Beck's therapy aims to identify the implicit and self-defeating assumptions depressed people make about themselves, change their validity and substitute more adaptive assumptions. Box 4.6 illustrates an exchange between a therapist using Beck's cognitive approach and a student who believed that she would not get into the college she had applied to.

Box 4.6 *Beck's approach to therapy in action*

Therapist: Why do you think you won't be able to get into the university of your choice?

Student: Because my grades were not really so hot.

Therapist: Well, what was your grade average?

Student: Well, pretty good up until the last semester in high school.

Therapist: What was your grade average in general?

Student: As and Bs.

Therapist: Well, how many of each?

Student: Well, I guess, almost all of my grades were As but I got terrible grades my last semester.

Therapist: What were your grades then?

Student: I got two As and two Bs.

Therapist: Since your grade average would seem to come out to almost all As, why do you think you won't be able to get into the university?

Student: Because of competition being so tough.

Therapist: Have you found out what the average grades are for admissions to the college?

Student: Well, somebody told me that a B+ average would suffice.

Therapist: Isn't your average better than that?

Student: I guess so.

(From Beck *et al.*, 1979)

Note how the therapist attempts to reverse the 'catastrophising beliefs' held by the student concerning herself, her situation and her future. Note also how the therapist takes a gentler, less confrontational and more experiential approach to the student than a rational–emotive therapist would.

Box 4.6 illustrates the strategy of identifying a person's self-impressions which, although not recognised as such, are misguided. Once the self-impressions have been identified, the therapist's role is to attempt to disprove rather than confirm the negative self-image (Williams, 1992). By sharing knowledge of the cognitive model, the person undergoing therapy may then understand the origins of the disorder and ultimately develop skills to apply effective interventions independently.

Given its original purpose, it is not surprising that Beck's approach to therapy is most successful in treating depression (Andrews, 1991). However, the therapy has also been used successfully with eating disorders (Fairburn *et al.*, 1993). Whether Beck's approach can be applied to schizophrenia and personality disorders is the subject of much debate (Beck & Freeman, 1990; Tarrier *et al.*, 1993).

Attributional therapy

Attributional therapy is a relatively recent cognitive approach to the treatment of depression, which derives from the research concerning the revised theory of *learned helplessness*. Attributions are our beliefs about the causes of our own and other people's behaviours (see Gross & McIlveen, 1998). Attributional therapists hold that, in some cases, depressed people make unrealistic or faulty attributions concerning their own behaviours and that these can cause considerable distress.

When asked to explain successful or unsuccessful outcomes, most people show the *self-serving bias*. However, this is reversed in depressed people, who attribute failures to internal causes, even when there is no evidence to support such an attribution. Successful outcomes, by contrast, tend to be attributed to external causes. For example, a depressed individual who passes an examination may attribute the success to 'an easy examination paper that anybody could have passed', when in fact it was the individual's own ability that produced the positive outcome.

Attributional therapists attempt to break the vicious circle that people low in self-esteem experience. This involves training them to perceive successes as resulting from internal factors and at least some failures from external factors beyond their control. Changing attributions can result in increased self-esteem, greater confidence and better performance. Moreover, beneficial changes can occur after only a small number of therapy sessions, which is clearly advantageous (Brockner & Guare, 1983).

Box 4.7   *Attributional therapy and depression*

Rabin *et al.* (1986) gave 235 depressed adults a ten-session programme that initially explained the advantages of interpreting events in the way that non-depressed people do. After this, they were trained to reform their habitually negative patterns of thinking and labelling by, for example, being given 'homework assignments', in which they recorded each day's positive events and the contributions they had made to them. Compared with a group of depressed people given no programme, the group receiving the ten-session programme reported experiencing significantly less depression.

Meichenbaum's stress inoculation therapy

Meichenbaum's (1976, 1985) *stress inoculation therapy* assumes that people sometimes find situations stressful because they think about them in catastrophising ways. Stress inoculation therapy aims to train people to cope more effectively with potentially stressful situations. The therapy consists of three stages. The first, *cognitive preparation* (or *conceptualisation*) involves the therapist and person exploring the way in which stressful situations are thought about. Typically, people react to stress by offering negative self-statements like 'I can't handle this'. This exacerbates an already stressful situation. The second stage, *skill acquisition and rehearsal*, attempts to replace negative self-statements with incompatible positive coping statements. These are then learned and practised.

Box 4.8 *Some coping and reinforcing self-statements used in stress inoculation therapy*

Preparing for a stressful situation
- What is it you have to do?
- You can develop a plan to deal with it.
- Just think about what you can do about it; that's better than getting anxious.
- No negative self-statements; just think rationally.
- Don't worry; worry won't help anything.
- Maybe what you think is anxiety is eagerness to confront it.

Confronting and handling a stressful situation
- Just 'psych' yourself up – you can meet this challenge.
- One step at a time; you can handle the situation.
- Don't think about fear; just think about what you have to do. Stay relevant.
- This anxiety is what the therapist said you would feel. It's a reminder to use your coping exercises.
- This tenseness can be an ally, a cue to cope.
- Relax; you're in control. Take a slow deep breath.
- Ah, good.

Coping with the feeling of being overwhelmed
- When fear comes, just pause.
- Keep the focus on the present; what is it that you have to do?
- Label your fear from 0 to 10 and watch it change.
- You should expect your fear to rise.
- Don't try to eliminate fear totally; just keep it manageable.
- You can convince yourself to do it. You can reason fear away.
- It will be over shortly.
- It's not the worst thing that can happen.
- Just think about something else.
- Do something that will prevent you from thinking about fear.
- Describe what is around you. That way you won't think about worrying.

Reinforcing self-statements
- It worked; you did it.
- Wait until you tell your therapist about this.
- It wasn't as bad as you expected.
- You made more out of the fear than it was worth.
- Your damn ideas – that's the problem. When you control them, you control your fear.

> ● **It's getting better each time you use the procedures.**
> ● **You can be pleased with the progress you're making.**
> ● **You did it!**
> **(From Meichenbaum, 1976)**

The final stage of therapy, *application and follow-through*, involves the therapist guiding the person through progressively more threatening situations that have been rehearsed in actual stress-producing situations. Initially, the person is placed in a situation that is moderately easy to cope with. Once this has been mastered, a more difficult situation is presented. According to Meichenbaum *et al.* (1982), the 'power of positive thinking' approach advocated by stress inoculation therapy can be successful in bringing about effective behaviour change, particularly in relation to anxiety and pain.

Some other applications of therapies derived from the cognitive model

Like other therapies, therapies based on the cognitive model have received considerable scrutiny as to their worth (Andrews, 1993). Cognitively based therapies can be particularly helpful in the treatment of *panic disorder*. Clark (1993) has argued that the core disturbance in this disorder is an abnormality in thinking, in which people interpret normal bodily signs and symptoms as indications of an impending mental or physical catastrophe (such as a heart attack). Because of their fears, people become *hypervigilant* and repeatedly scan their body for signs of danger, which results in their noticing sensations that other people would not be aware of. Additionally, subtle *avoidance behaviours* prevent them from disconfirming their negative beliefs. For example, people convinced that they are suffering from cardiac disease may avoid exercise and rest whenever a palpitation occurs, in the belief that this will prevent a fatal heart attack.

Clark *et al.* (1994) and Shear *et al.* (1994) have shown that cognitively based therapies can be highly effective in changing the cognitions and behaviour of 90 per cent of those treated. However, whether therapies derived from the cognitive model can and should be used with other disorders is less clear-cut. For example, in a review of research concerning obsessive–compulsive disorder, James & Blackburn (1995) found that of the few well-controlled studies examining cognitively based therapies' effectiveness, there was little evidence to suggest that improvement occurred. Against that, however, are findings indicating that cognitively based therapies can have a significant impact on many medical conditions such as chronic fatigue syndrome (Sharpe *et al.*, 1996) and in reducing the psychological impact of unemployment (Proudfoot *et al.*, 1997).

Conclusions

Therapies based on the cognitive model have been used to treat several types of mental disorder, particularly depression. Although useful in the treatment of this disorder, their usefulness with other disorders is less clear-cut.

Summary

- Therapies based on the cognitive model attempt to show people that their distorted/irrational thoughts are the main contributors to their disorder. By changing faulty thinking, disorders can be alleviated.
- Bandura's approach to therapy uses **modelling**. As well as changing behaviour, models aim to change thoughts and perceptions. Modelling is useful in the treatment of phobias and is also effective in **assertiveness** and **social skills training**. One reason for this is the development of **self-efficacy**.
- Ellis sees emotional difficulties as a result of 'irrational beliefs'. People have the capacity for rational understanding, but are also capable of deluding themselves and thinking irrationally.

Rational–emotive therapy (RET) aims to help people find flaws in their thinking by creating a **dispute belief system**.

- When irrational beliefs have been identified, they are substituted by more realistic ones. RET is an active, direct and argumentative approach, which has been questioned by those who stress **empathy**'s importance in therapy. However, it seems to be effective for certain disorders.

- Beck's **cognitive restructuring therapy** also sees disorders as stemming from irrational beliefs. The therapy is specifically designed to treat **depression**, and is effective in this. In a less confrontational way than RET, it identifies depressed people's implicit and self-defeating assumptions.

- **Attributional therapy** is derived from the revised theory of learned helplessness and also treats depression. Attributional therapists try to break down the vicious circles that low self-esteem people experience. Changing attributions like this can lead to increased self-esteem, greater confidence and better performance.

- Meichenbaum's **stress inoculation therapy** assumes that people sometimes find situations stressful because of their misperceptions about them. The therapy trains people to cope more effectively with potentially stressful situations through **cognitive preparation**, **skill acquisition** and **rehearsal**, and **application** and **practice**.

- Cognitively based therapies are particularly helpful in treating **panic disorder**. They have also been shown to have a significant impact on many medical conditions and to reduce the psychological impact of unemployment. Their effectiveness with other disorders is, however, less clear-cut.

THERAPIES BASED ON THE HUMANISTIC MODEL

Introduction and overview

5

The humanistic model sees people as *sets of potentials* who are basically 'good' and strive for growth, dignity and self-determination. Mental disorders arise when external factors somehow block the potential for personal growth. Therapies based on the humanistic model attempt to remove such blocks and put people 'in touch' with their true selves. This chapter examines some of the therapeutic approaches based on the humanistic model. It considers Rogers' *client-* (or *person-*) *centred therapy*, Perls' *Gestalt therapy* and some humanistic approaches to *group therapy*.

Rogers' client- (or person-) centred therapy

Humanistic therapy was introduced in the 1940s by Rogers (1951), who originally called his approach *client-centred therapy*. However, in 1974, he and his colleagues changed its name to *person-centred therapy*, in order to focus more clearly on the human values the approach emphasises (Meador & Rogers, 1984). The therapy was also called *non-directive therapy*, because Rogers refused to tell people what to do or think (but see also page 75). Instead of directing therapy, the Rogerian approach is to clarify feelings by rephrasing what people say and repeatedly asking what they really believe and feel. Rather than looking at earlier parts of life, Rogers believed in focusing on the present.

Many people regard it as unusual for a therapist to refuse to offer expert advice. For example, a woman who sought advice on what to tell her daughter about relationships with men was repeatedly asked by Rogers what *she* thought. After several direct questions, Rogers replied:

'I feel this is the kind of very private thing that I couldn't possibly answer for you, but I sure as anything will try to help you work towards your own answer' (Meador & Rogers, 1973).

For Rogers (1986), the central premise of person-centred therapy is that:

'the individual has within him or herself vast resources of self-understanding, for altering his or her self-concept, attitudes and self-directing behaviour, and ... these resources can be tapped if only a definable climate of facilitative psychological attitudes can be provided'.

Encouraging personal growth

There are three major elements in the 'definable climate' or 'therapeutic atmosphere' which Rogers believed would encourage personal growth in his clients. These are *genuineness, unconditional positive regard* and *empathy*.

Genuineness

Genuineness (or *authenticity* or *congruence*) refers to real human relationships in which therapists honestly express their own feelings. According to Rogers, it would be harmful to clients if a therapist could not be 'dependably real', that is, truly accept and like them, even though their values might differ from the therapist's. Therapists who tried to manufacture a fake concern or hide their own beliefs would actually *impede* their clients' true personal growth. Rogers admitted that he sometimes had negative feelings about his clients. The most common feeling was boredom, and he expressed this rather than holding it in (Bennett, 1985). If the therapist says one thing, but somehow communicates a different feeling, the client will pick this up and believe the therapist cannot be trusted.

Box 5.1 *Genuineness*

Rogers (1980) sees genuineness as the most important of the three elements:

'Sometimes [in therapy] a feeling 'rises up in me' which seems to have no particular relationship to what is going on. Yet I have

---

learned to accept and trust this feeling in my awareness and to try to communicate it to my client. For example, a client is talking to me, and I suddenly feel an image of him as a pleading little boy, folding his hands in supplication, saying 'Please let me have this, please let me have this'. I have learned that if I can be real in the relationship with him and express this feeling that has occurred in me, it is very likely to strike some deep note in him and advance our relationship.'

Unconditional positive regard

This means respecting clients as important human beings with values and goals, and accepting people for what they are without reservation. Rogers believed that therapists should not judge clients' worth by their behaviours. Rather, they should provide a sense of security that encourages clients to follow their own feelings and recognise each person's essential dignity. Therapists must, therefore, convince clients that they actually like and respect them, and that the positive regard they give does not depend on what the client says or does.

Empathy

Empathy (or *empathic understanding*) is the process of perceiving the world from the client's perspective and understanding what he or she is experiencing. It is not to be confused with sympathy. For example, a therapist who says, 'I'm sorry you feel insecure', may be genuine, but not empathic, because empathy involves an attempt to 'get inside the client's head' and to fully understand why the client lacks security. Thus, the client must be convinced that he or she is *understood* by the therapist. Without such understanding, a client might think, 'Sure, this therapist says he likes me and respects me, but that's because he really doesn't know me. If he really knew me, he wouldn't like me'.

Box 5.2 *Empathic understanding*

Client: I was thinking about this business of standards. I somehow developed a sort of knack, I guess, of, well, habit, of trying to make people feel at ease around me, or to make things go along smoothly.

Therapist: In other words, what you did was always in the direction of trying to keep things smooth and to make other people feel better and to smooth the situation.

Client: Yes. I think that's what it was. Now the reason why I did it probably was – I mean, not that I was a good little Samaritan going around making other people happy, but that was probably the role that felt easiest for me to play. I'd been doing it around the home so much. I just didn't stand up for my own convictions, until I don't know whether I have any convictions to stand up for.

Therapist: You feel that for a long time you've been playing the role of kind of smoothing out the frictions or differences or what not ...

Client: Mm-hmm.

Therapist: Rather than having any opinion or reaction of your own in the situation. Is that it?

Client: That's it. Or that I haven't been really honestly being myself, or actually knowing what my real self is, and that I've been playing a sort of false role. Whatever role no one else was playing, and that needed to be played at the time, I'd try to fill it in.

(From Rogers,1951)

Genuineness, unconditional positive regard and empathy are interconnected. Changes in a client's moment-to-moment feelings require that the therapist accepts and values the client (shows both empathy and unconditional positive regard). As noted, genuineness is the most important of all, because a meaningful relationship demands that empathy and unconditional positive regard are honest and real.

Techniques used in Rogerian therapy

Typically, Rogerian therapy sessions are held once a week with the client and therapist facing each other. One way of achieving empathic understanding is through *active listening,* in which the therapist attempts to grasp both the *content* of what the client says and the *feeling* behind it. To communicate empathy, the therapist uses *reflection*, summarising the client's message (in terms of its content and feeling) and *feeding* this back. For example, a client who says 'I'm depressed', might have the therapist respond with 'Sounds like you're really down'.

Although empathy requires a great deal of skill, Rogers (1986) sees active listening as 'one of the most potent forces for change that I know'. As well as helping clients understand or clarify their feelings, active listening also lets them know that the therapist both understands and accepts what is being said. According to Thorne (1984), empathy is the most 'trainable' of the three major elements, but is also remarkably rare. As noted previously, therapists do not offer direct advice or interpretations, but may ask for clarifications now and again.

The therapist's passive reflection is gradually replaced by *active interpretation*. By going beyond the overt content of what the client says, the therapist responds to what is sensed to be the client's true feelings. The therapist starts to confront the client with inconsistencies in what is said, and may, for example, point out that the client is failing to take responsibility for personal actions.

In an atmosphere where anything that is felt may be expressed, the focus is more on *present* than past feelings. During therapy, clients begin to realise that, perhaps for the first time, someone is listening to them, and they become more aware of long-denied feelings and thoughts, and learn to accept these and incorporate them into their self-concept. In Rogers' terms, clients 'get it together' and experience *congruence*.

Application and evaluation of Rogerian therapy

As well as being used with individuals, Rogerian therapy is also used in human relations training for professionals of all kinds, including nurses, crisis workers and counsellors. In universities, for example, the approach has been used with students who have not yet made career choices. The therapy helps decision-making by providing an encouraging atmosphere in which clients can explore various choices and paths. As noted, Rogerian therapists do not tell clients what to do, but help them to arrive at their own decisions.

Box 5.3   *Client-centred therapy in action*

Client: I guess I do have problems at school ... You see, I'm the chairman of the Science department, so you can imagine what kind of a department it is.

Therapist: You sort of feel that if *you're* in something that it can't be too good. Is that ...?

Client: Well, it's not that I ... It's just that I'm ... I don't think that I could run it.

Therapist: You don't have any confidence in yourself?

Client: No confidence, no confidence in myself. I never had any confidence in myself. I – like I told you that – like when even when I was a kid, I didn't feel I was capable and I always wanted to get back with the intellectual group.

Therapist: This has been a long-term thing, then. It's gone on a long time.

Client: Yeah, the *feeling* is – even though I know it isn't, it's the feeling that I have, that I haven't got it, that ... that ... that ... people will find out that I'm dumb or ... or ...

Therapist: Masquerade ...

Client: Superficial, I'm just superficial. There's nothing below the surface. Just superficial generalities, that ...

Therapist: There's nothing really deep and meaningful to you.

Client: No – they don't know it, and ...

Therapist: And you're terrified they're going to find out.

Client: My wife has a friend, and – and she and the friend got together so we could go out together with her and my wife and her husband ... And the guy, he's an engineer and he's, you know – he's got it, you know; and I don't want to go, I don't want to go because ... because if ... if we get together he's liable to start to ... to talk about something I don't know, and I'll ... I won't know about that.

Therapist: You're terribly frightened in this sort of thing.

Client: I ... I'm afraid to be around people who ... who I feel are my peers. Even in pool ... now I ... I play pool very well and ... if I'm playing with some guy that I ... I know I can beat, *psychologically*, I can run 50, but ... but if I start playing with somebody that's my

---

> level, I'm done. I'm done. I ... I ... I'll miss a ball every time.
> **Therapist:** So the ... the fear of what's going on just immobilises
> you, keeps you from doing a good job.
> (From Hersher, 1970)

Rogers & Dymond (1954) published studies detailing person-centered therapy's success. Unlike supporters of some other therapies who rely on their own judgements, Rogers recorded therapeutic sessions so that his techniques could be evaluated. Truax (1966) obtained permission from Rogers and his clients to record therapy sessions in order to determine their effectiveness. Truax found that only those clients who showed progress were regularly followed by positive responses from Rogers, and that during their therapy, they made more statements indicating progress.

What this suggests is that social reinforcement is very powerful. This does not discredit client-centred therapy, but shows that Rogers was very effective in adopting a strategy for altering a person's behaviour. Although the term *non-directive* was initially used to describe Rogerian therapy, when Rogers realised he was reinforcing positive statements, he stopped referring to it as non-directive, because it quite clearly was not.

Box 5.4 *Q-sorts*

One method used by Rogers to validate client-centred therapy empirically was the *Q-sort*. This consists of cards which have statements relating to the self, such as 'I am a domineering person'. Clients are required to arrange them in a series of ten piles ranging from 'very characteristic of me' to 'not at all characteristic of me' to describe the self-image. The process is then repeated to describe the 'ideal self'. After this, the two Q-sorts are correlated to determine the discrepancy between actual self-image and ideal self-image. During therapy, the procedure is repeated several times, the idea being that if therapy is having a beneficial effect, the discrepancy between actual self-image and ideal self-image should narrow (and the correlation between them increase).

Critics of Rogerian therapy have objected to its methods on the grounds that it treats people in the same way irrespective of their disorder (a point which also applies to some other therapies). It has also been suggested that giving people unconditional positive regard might actually be harmful, because they could leave therapy with the unrealistic expectation that anything they do will meet with society's approval (Bandura, 1969). Also, Rogerian therapy is not appropriate for disorders like schizophrenia, and seems to be most effective for people who want to change, and who are intelligent enough to gain some sort of insight concerning their problems.

Other critics have argued that the humanistic model is simply wrong in viewing humans as being basically 'good'. Whether a person who has exhibited signs of dissocial personality disorder should be provided with unconditional positive regard is debatable. The therapy is, however, more affordable and less time-consuming than, say, psychodynamic therapies.

According to Barker (1998), the core emphasis on the experience of mental distress has found its way into almost all contemporary therapies through working in the 'here and now'. This legacy:

'... will live on, long after many other forms of popular therapy have been consigned to the footnotes of history'.

Perls' Gestalt therapy

Like Rogers, Perls believed that therapy should help people integrate conflicting parts of their personalities. Perls was dissatisfied with psychoanalysis and called it 'a disease that pretends to be a cure'. However, whilst Perls agreed with Rogers that people are free to make choices and affect their growth, Gestalt therapy is highly *directive*, and the therapist leads the client through *planned experiences*.

Despite his dissatisfaction with psychoanalysis, Perls agreed with Freud that mental disorders result from unconscious conflicts and, like Freud, he stressed the importance of dream analysis. However, whereas Freud saw dreams as the 'royal road to the unconscious', Perls saw them as 'disowned parts of the personality'. Another difference between them was that Perls believed current problems (the 'here and now') could be focused on, and that people have responsibility for the direction of their own lives (which is, of course, consistent with the humanistic model).

Perls called his therapy Gestalt therapy, referring to the German word that means 'pattern' or 'organised whole', because he believed that when therapy was complete, a person became 'whole' and could resume normal growth. The approach was particularly influential in the 1960s, especially in the USA. According to Gestalt therapists, psychologically healthy people are aware of themselves so fully that they can detect whatever requires their attention. Mental disorders occur as a result of a blockage of awareness. Perls saw awareness as being critical, because if people are unaware of what they want or feel at any time or moment, then they have limited control over their feelings and behaviours. At times, we act out of habit rather than choice, and the habits may become self-defeating.

Figure 5.1 *Frederick (Fritz) Perls (1893–1970), founder of Gestalt therapy*

Gestalt therapists, then, see mental disorders as arising because the various aspects of personality (such as thoughts, feelings and actions) cannot be integrated into a healthy, well-organised whole. The aim of therapy is, therefore, to help a person bring together the 'alienated fragments' of the self into an integrated, unified whole (the sense of wholeness is called *organismic self-regulation*). Gestalt therapists believe that by achieving a sense of wholeness, people can relate more fully to others and live more spontaneous lives.

The development of awareness allows an individual to confront and make choices, an assumption being that when allowed to make choices, people choose self-enhancing and growthful options instead of self-defeating ones that have been used before. So, by being aware of inner conflicts, people can accept reality, rather than deny and repress it. This can help productive choices to be made, despite misgivings and fear.

Gestalt therapy's primary focus is on moment-to-moment *self-awareness*. The therapist's role is that of an *active co-explorer* with clients, encouraging them to break through whatever defences are preventing full experience of their feelings and thoughts. The client–therapist relationship has been likened to that between an apprentice and master (Kempler, 1973). The skill the master teaches the apprentice is that of awareness. As the relationship between them develops, the therapist uses awareness to enhance growth in the client.

Perls did not believe there was any set formula for achieving this. However, Levitsky & Perls (1970) provided guidelines for therapists. In many ways, Gestalt therapists behave like psychoanalysts by, for example, directing clients' attention to conflicts and dreams. But as noted, Gestalt therapists interpret dreams differently. For them, fragments of dreams are aspects of personality, and the aim is to help clients piece together dream fragments as they relate to current problems.

Typically, therapy is conducted in a *group setting* (see page 82) with the focus on one person at a time. Various techniques are used to help people become aware of who they are and what they are feeling, and of personal responsibility. According to Gestalt therapists, any action implies a choice, and with choice goes responsibility. On some occasions, a therapist will deliberately frustrate clients, especially if clients are trying to lean on the therapist when support is not really necessary. The therapist's job is to emphasise awareness on the client's part, and this can be achieved in various ways.

Box 5.5 *Some techniques used in Gestalt therapy*

The following techniques or 'directed experiments' are usually carried out in a consulting room or group setting.

Role playing: A person who is angry at his or her mother, say, first plays him- or herself talking to the mother and then reverses the roles and becomes the mother. In the *empty chair exercise*, the client moves back and forth between two chairs to play the roles. Perls believed that by acting out both sides to a conflict, a person would complete *unfinished business*, that is, become aware of unexpressed *feelings* that had been carried around for many years. This allows a sense of completion to be gained, which frees the individual to deal with present-day problems rather than those from the past. Note how different this is to Rogers' therapy. Indeed, unlike a Rogerian, a Gestalt therapist might even become involved and join in the role playing.

Amplification: The therapist asks the client to exaggerate some behaviour or feeling in order to become more aware of it. A man who responds to a question about his wife, for example, might talk favourably about her, but draw his fingers towards his palm slightly. When asked to exaggerate this, the client might make a fist, strike the table and offer revealing comments about his wife.

Dialogue: In this, the client undertakes verbal confrontations between opposing wishes and ideas. One example of clashing personality elements is *underdog* and *top dog*. The former, and its suggestions of 'don't take chances' is confronted with the latter and its suggestions that 'you'll never progress if you don't take chances'. A heightened awareness of the elements of conflict can clear the path towards resolution, perhaps through compromise.

Speaking in the first person: This approach helps people recognise and take responsibility for their own actions. A person who says 'sometimes people are afraid to take the first step in initiating

---

> a relationship for fear of being rejected' is encouraged to restate this in the first person: '*I* am afraid to take the first step ... because *I* fear being rejected'.

The ultimate aim of therapy is to make people aware of their problems, and teach them *how* to become aware, so they can do this independently. When this has been achieved, therapy is complete.

Box 5.6   *The moral injunctions of Gestalt therapy*

- Live now. Be concerned with the present rather than the past or future.
- Live here. Deal with what is present rather than what is absent.
- Stop imagining. Experience the real.
- Stop unnecessary thinking. Rather, taste and see.
- Express rather than manipulate, explain, justify or judge.
- Give in to unpleasantness and pain just as to pleasure. Do not restrict your awareness.
- Accept no 'should' or 'ought' other than your own. Adore no graven image.
- Take full responsibility for your actions, feelings and thoughts.
- Surrender to being as you are.

One way of evaluating Gestalt therapy's effectiveness and appropriateness is in terms of the number of people who have adopted it. Proponents argue that its growth is one indicator of its effectiveness. However, there have been few controlled studies to validate Gestalt therapy, and so it is not known how effective it is (Rimm & Masters, 1979). Gestalt therapists argue that controlled research is not necessary, because the direct experiences of those who have received it are overwhelming evidence of its effectiveness. Moreover, because the therapy is so individualised, it cannot be evaluated in the same way as other therapies (a point returned to in Chapter 6). Evidence suggests, however, that techniques like amplification can be effective (Simkin & Yontef, 1984), though clearly Gestalt therapy, like other therapies, is more effective with some populations than others.

Humanistic approaches to group therapy

Although group approaches to therapy were described in Chapter 2, the humanistic model has contributed most to the group therapy movement. The major therapeutic gains of group approaches are believed to be the development of intimacy and co-operation through being part of a mutually supportive group, and finding out about oneself through candid interactions with others.

Encounter groups

The earliest form of *humanistic group therapy* (which laboured under the generic term *human potential movement*) was the *encounter group*, part of the American (and, in particular, Californian) culture of the 1960s and 1970s. Encounter groups were originally developed by Rogers to be what Graham (1986) has called:

> 'a means whereby people can break through the barriers erected by themselves and others in order to react openly and freely with one another'.

Participants (as opposed to *clients*) are encouraged to act out their emotions, rather than just talk about them, through bodily contact and structured 'games'. The group leader (or *facilitator*) attempts to create an atmosphere of mutual trust in which group members, usually numbering between eight and 18, feel free to express their feelings irrespective of whether these are positive or negative. According to Rogers (1973), this expression reduces defensiveness and promotes self-actualisation.

Sensitivity training groups

Sensitivity training groups (or *T-groups*) were first introduced in the late 1940s with the intention of helping group leaders improve the functioning of groups by democratic methods. Later, the approach was used to help business executives improve their relations with co-workers. Unlike encounter groups, in which feelings are expressed by yelling, weeping, touching exercises, and other unrestrained displays of emotion, T-groups were originally limited to 'subtler' emotional expressions. However, whether such groups can bring about change is questionable, and some have warned against their dangers.

It has been claimed that such groups can precipitate, if not cause, various sorts of psychological disturbances. Aggressive, highly charismatic and authoritarian leaders were the most likely to have 'casualties' (people who suffered a severe psychological disturbance lasting up to six months after the group experience). One destructive characteristic is the pressure to have some ecstatic (what Maslow, 1968, calls *peak*) experience, which is viewed as necessary for continuing mental health. Maslow himself, however, would argue that such experiences are relatively uncommon and certainly cannot be produced 'on demand'.

Box 5.7 *T-groups, encounter groups and Gestalt therapy*

It was noted on page 78 that Gestalt therapy is typically conducted in a group setting with the focus on one person at a time. However, in its pure group form, participants in Gestalt therapy *help one another* work through their emotional crises. Unlike T-groups, but like encounter groups, unrestrained emotional outpouring is encouraged, with emphasis on the participants' present experiences. For Perls (1967), such group approaches are helpful because: 'in the safe emergency of the therapeutic situation, the (individual) discovers that the world does not fall to pieces if he or she gets angry, sexy, jealous or mournful'.

Conclusions

Therapies based on the humanistic model of abnormality aim to put people in touch with their true selves. They have attracted considerable interest, and evidence suggests that they can be effective in the treatment of certain disorders.

Summary

- Humanistic therapies aim to remove blocks to personal growth and put people 'in touch' with their true selves. Rogers' **client/person-centred therapy** involves clarifying feelings by repeating what people say and repeatedly asking what they really believe/feel **without** offering any expert advice.

- The three major elements which Rogers believes encourage personal growth are **genuineness (authenticity/congruence)**, **unconditional positive regard** and **empathy**. Of these, genuineness is the most important, because a meaningful relationship demands that empathy and unconditional positive regard are honest and real.

- Rogerian therapy typically involves a once-weekly session, with client and therapist facing each other. Passive reflection is gradually replaced by **active interpretation**, in which the therapist goes beyond the overt content of what the client says and responds to the client's true feelings. The outcome of this is **congruence**.

- Evaluations of Rogers' therapy indicate that social reinforcement by the therapist is a very powerful strategy for changing people's behaviour. This does not discredit the therapy, but shows that it is not non-directive. Another way of evaluating the therapy is through **Q-sorts**.

- Rogerian therapy is not helpful in disorders like schizophrenia. It is most effective with people who want to change and are capable of gaining insight into their problems. It is also much more affordable and less time-consuming than psychodynamic approaches.

- **Gestalt therapy** also tries to help people integrate conflicting parts of their personalities. However, it is highly **directive** and the therapist leads the client through 'planned experiences'. Mental disorders are seen as blockages of **awareness**. Therapy tries to bring together the 'alienated fragments' of the self into an integrated, unified whole (**organismic self-regulation**).

- There is no set formula for achieving awareness. Therapy usually takes place in a **group setting,** with the focus on one person at a time. Various techniques ('directed experiments') are used. These include **role playing**, **amplification**, **dialogue** and **speaking-in-the-first-person**.
- The ultimate aim of Gestalt therapy is to teach people **how** to become aware of their problems, so they can deal with them independently. The **moral injunctions** of Gestalt therapy are rules to live one's life by.
- The humanistic model has contributed more than any other to **group therapy** (the **human potential movement**). Rogers developed **encounter groups,** in which participants are encouraged to act out their positive and negative emotions through bodily contact and structured 'games'. The 'facilitator' creates an air of mutual trust.
- **Sensitivity training groups** (**T-groups**) were originally intended to help group leaders improve group functioning by democratic methods. However, their effectiveness in producing change has been questioned, and critics claim that they may actually cause mental disturbances.

ASSESSING THE EFFECTIVENESS OF THERAPIES

Introduction and overview

6

Chapters 1–5 described therapeutic approaches that either have been or currently are used to treat mental disorders. Although the procedures and disorders they are used with were described in detail, their effectiveness was not. This chapter looks at attempts to assess the effectiveness of therapies and considers major issues surrounding such attempts.

Early attempts at assessing therapy's effectiveness

Eysenck (1952) made the first systematic attempt to evaluate therapy's effectiveness. He examined psychoanalysis and *eclectic* psychotherapy (psychotherapy incorporating a variety of approaches, rather than the single approach used in psycho-analysis). Prior to Eysenck's findings being published, the value and effectiveness of psychotherapeutic approaches had not been seriously questioned since, at least as far as therapists were concerned, many people seeking treatment improved and reported themselves satisfied with its effects.

Box 6.1 *Eysenck's assessment of therapy's effectiveness*

According to Eysenck, Freudian therapeutic approaches were 'unsupported by any scientifically acceptable evidence'. Looking at studies conducted between 1920 and 1951, Eysenck discovered that in only 44 per cent of cases using psychoanalysis could the person be considered 'cured', 'much improved' or 'improved'. Using the same criteria to assess people treated by means of eclectic psy-chotherapy, the figure was higher, at 64 per cent.

Eysenck argued that many people with psychological problems actually improve without any professional treatment (*spontaneous remission*). To assess the effectiveness of the two psychotherapies, it was necessary to compare the above figures with a *control group* of people with similar problems to those who received therapy, but who did not themselves receive any form of professional treatment (by, for example, being treated only custodially in an institution). Eysenck located two such studies (Landis, 1938; Denker, 1946) and found that 66 per cent satisfied the 'cured', 'much improved' or 'improved' criteria. On the basis of these data, he concluded that:

'There thus appears to be an inverse correlation between recovery and psychotherapy: the more psychotherapy, the smaller the recovery rate'.

Eysenck's claim that no treatment is at least as effective, if not more effective, than professional treatment was not greeted enthusiastically by psychoanalysts or eclectic psychotherapists. Nor was his additional claim that it was unethical for therapists to charge people for their services, when the evidence suggested they were paying for nothing (Eysenck, 1992).

Following the publication of Eysenck's controversial article, several critiques were made of his conclusions and much research was conducted on assessing therapy's effectiveness. For example, some researchers questioned Eysenck's inclusion as 'failures' those people who 'dropped out' of therapy, on the grounds that somebody who leaves therapy cannot necessarily be counted as 'not cured'. When Eysenck's figures were reanalysed taking this into account, the figure of 44 per cent for psychoanalysis rose to a considerably higher 66 per cent (Oatley, 1984).

Other researchers argued that the success rate for psycho-analysis increased to 83 per cent if 'improvement' was measured differently (Bergin, 1971). Yet others argued that the people in Eysenck's 'control' group differed in important ways from those who received treatment (a point acknowledged by Eysenck). Malan *et al.* (1975), for example, noted that 'untreated' individuals actually had one assessment interview, which some of them perceived as a powerful impetus for *self-induced change*. Since the interview clearly influenced at least some people, they could hardly be considered to have 'spontaneously' recovered. Even Landis (1938), whose article was one of those from which Eysenck derived his figure for spontaneous remission, noted that there were differences between those who received therapy and those who did not.

The issue of measurement

To evaluate a therapy, it is clearly necessary to have some way of *measuring* its effectiveness, that is, there should be a *criterion of success* (Crooks & Stein, 1991). Unfortunately, it is not easy to determine what the most appropriate criterion should be. Some therapists would argue that the most appropriate and straight-forward measurement is an observable change in behaviour. After all, if a person has a phobia before a course of therapy begins but does not have one after it has ended, then the therapy has surely been successful (Guscott & Taylor, 1994).

Those who use therapies based on the behavioural model (see Chapter 3) define their therapeutic goals in such terms, and would certainly want observable change to be used as the criterion of success. However, with some other therapies, this criterion would be considered inappropriate. Psychoanalysts argue that for therapy to be effective, unconscious conflicts must be resolved and a restructuring of personality produced (see Chapter 2). Since these cannot be directly measured, psychoanalysts would argue that an observable change in behaviour cannot be the *only* criterion of success (Krebs & Blackman, 1988).

Box 6.2 *The problem of therapist bias*

Even if behaviour change were an appropriate criterion, *who* should be the judge of whether such a change has occurred? To use the therapist would surely be a mistake. What therapist, who has seen a person over a long period of time (and in all probability receiving payment), would conclude that therapy has been ineffec-tive? Therapists clearly have a stake in believing that their therapies are positive and they cannot possibly be unbiased.

Being unable to directly measure outcomes, psychoanalysts would argue that their analysands' reports must be relied on. However, this assumes that people are always excellent judges of their own behaviours, an assumption unlikely to be true. Moreover, since the insights gained in psychoanalysis are, by their nature, unique, it is impossible to measure objectively how much insight has been gained.

Using the family and friends of the person who has received treatment is also problematic, since in at least some cases, family members and/or friends may actually be the *cause* of a person's problems! Consider, for example, a woman who has sought therapy to be more assertive but is married to an overbearing husband. The husband would hardly be expected to approve of his previously submissive wife's increased assertiveness (Krebs & Blackman, 1988).

Perhaps the most objective assessors would be therapists who were not involved in an individual's treatment and who would, presumably, not be biased in their judgements. This approach was used by Sloane *et al.* (1975), who compared the effectiveness of psychotherapy, behaviour therapy and no therapy at all. The participants were 90 people suffering from various anxiety and personality disorders. They were carefully matched according to age, sex and their mental disorders, and then randomly assigned to a course of psychotherapy, behaviour therapy or were placed on a waiting list for therapy without actually receiving any treatment.

Highly experienced clinicians, who were experts in either psychotherapy or behaviour therapy, interviewed the participants before the study began and, without knowing which group they had been assigned to, at various times later on. After four months, 80 per cent of those treated using behaviour therapy or psychotherapy had either improved or recovered. For the control group, the figure was 48 per cent, suggesting that, contrary to Eysenck's (1952) claim, psychotherapy *did* have a significant effect compared with no treatment at all.

When the participants were assessed one year later, those treated with psychotherapy or behaviour therapy had maintained their improvement, whereas control group participants had made small but significant gains towards the levels of the two treatment groups. So, whilst spontaneous remission may occur (as Eysenck had claimed), both of the therapeutic techniques were still better than no treatment at all.

Box 6.3 *Experimental studies of the effectiveness of therapy – some important questions*

Although Sloane *et al.*'s (1975) study was methodologically sound, it raises several important questions. As noted, the participants were assigned to one of two therapeutic groups or a 'control' group. Suppose a similar study were conducted which extended over a lengthy time period, such as ten years. Should those in the 'control' group, who might (for example) be suicidal, be kept away from treatment? What if a person specifically sought out a particular therapy, but was assigned to either an alternative therapy or the control group?

In an ideal experiment, a person would be 'blind' to the therapy he or she was receiving to control for expectations about the treatment. Even if this could be done, would we really want to do it? Would it be ethical to deceive a person into thinking that another form of therapy was the same as the therapy being given?

Whilst carefully controlled research is essential, many important questions can be asked about this sort of research.

Durham *et al.* (1994) compared cognitive therapy, analytic psychotherapy and anxiety management training for *generalised anxiety disorder* (GAD) using an *assessor* who was 'blind' to the individual's therapist and treatment condition. Individuals were rated according to *symptom change*, a criterion devised by Jacobson *et al.* (1984) for determining the proportion of outpatients returning to normal functioning. Cognitive therapy was significantly more effective than analytic psychotherapy, with anxiety management training falling in between these two.

As well as an observable change in behaviour, many other measures could be used to assess a therapy's effectiveness. These include scores obtained on psychometric tests, and *recidivism rates* (whether or not a person is readmitted for therapy or seeks additional therapy in a period of time after an initial course has ended). Using these measures, Luborsky *et al.* (1975) claimed that improvements following a course of psychotherapy were significantly higher than in people who received no treatment at all. Luborsky *et al.* also reported that the outcome was better the more sessions that took place (the *dose–effect relationship*). However, because more treatment requires more time, the possibility that the mere passage of *time* contributes to improvement cannot be ruled out.

Meta-analytic studies

One way of overcoming the possibility that certain types of measurement may 'favour' certain therapies is to look at all types of measurement used by researchers. This approach was taken by Smith *et al.* (1980), who examined 475 studies concerned with therapy effectiveness. Some of these compared differences between therapies with respect to their effectiveness, whilst others compared a therapy's effectiveness against no treatment at all. Because researchers sometimes used several criteria of success, Smith *et al.* actually had 1776 outcome measures which varied from being highly subjective (some were supplied by therapists) to much more objective (the use of physiological measures).

Box 6.4   *Smith et al.'s (1980) meta-analysis*

The results of the 475 studies were analysed using *meta-analysis*. This allows researchers to *combine* the results from all of the studies conducted and produce an 'average estimate' of the size of effect of whatever is being investigated (Lilienfield, 1995). Those receiving therapy based on the psychodynamic model scored significantly higher on many criteria of success compared with those who received no treatment. However, there was considerable overlap in the outcomes for treated and untreated (control) individuals.

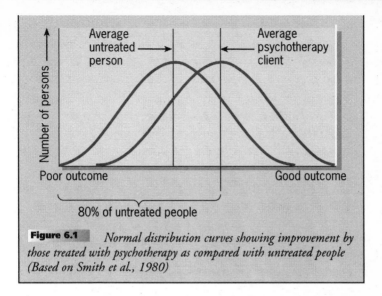

Figure 6.1 *Normal distribution curves showing improvement by those treated with psychotherapy as compared with untreated people (Based on Smith et al., 1980)*

On the basis of their findings, Smith *et al.* concluded that psychodynamic therapies are effective and that such therapies:

> 'benefit people of all ages as reliably as schooling educates them, medicine cures them or business turns a profit. The average person who receives therapy is better off at the end of it than 80 per cent of persons who do not'.

However, they also acknowledged that the case for psychotherapy's effectiveness was far from proven:

> 'This does not mean that everyone who receives psychotherapy improves. The evidence suggests that some people do not improve, and a small number get worse [Smith *et al.* report a figure of nine per cent]'.

Smith *et al.*'s conclusions were a far cry from Eysenck's (1965) remark that:

> 'current psychotherapeutic procedures have not lived up to the hopes which greeted their emergence 50 years ago'.

However, Smith *et al.*'s meta-analysis attracted considerable criticism. For example, over half the people receiving treatment in the 475 studies were *students*, who are hardly representative of the general population. Also, in some of the studies, the psychological problems being treated were not particularly serious, including smoking, overeating and performance anxieties (Shapiro & Shapiro, 1982).

More important was the inclusion of studies which were seriously methodologically flawed. In a reanalysis of the original meta-analysis, Prioleau *et al.* (1983) found only 32 studies free from methodological defects and otherwise sound. Analysis of these led Prioleau *et al.* to a different conclusion from that reached by Smith *et al.*:

> 'Thirty years after Eysenck first raised the issue of the effectiveness of psychotherapy ... and after about 500 outcome studies have been reviewed, we are still not aware of a single convincing demonstration [of] the benefits of psychotherapy'.

In a lengthy debate that followed Prioleau *et al.*'s reanalysis, those involved in assessing psychotherapy's effectiveness, including Eysenck and Smith, were invited to comment on the findings. The only thing agreed was that no agreement could be reached! The issue of psychotherapy's effectiveness has yet to be resolved. Some evidence suggests that psychotherapy can be at least as effective as chemotherapy in treating certain disorders (Garfield, 1992). Andrews (1993), by contrast, has argued that dynamic psychotherapy is no better than routine clinical care. In his view:

> 'The lack of evidence for efficacy despite considerable research, the real possibility of harm and the high cost all make dynamic psychotherapy unlikely to be a preferred option of the health service'.

Meta-analyses of research into the effectiveness of other therapies have also been conducted. Piccinelli *et al.* (1995) looked at the effectiveness of chemotherapy (see Chapter 1) in the treatment of obsessive–compulsive disorder (OCD). They found that with various outcome measures (such as *global clinical improvement* and psychosocial adjustment), drugs were far superior to *placebo* treatment (see Box 6.5), with non-SSRI antidepressant drugs (see Chapter 1) being by far the most effective in the short-term treatment of OCD.

Comparing the relative effectiveness of therapies

We have encountered several studies which, at least in part, aimed to compare the effectiveness of various therapies. Another study of this sort was conducted by May (1975), who assigned schizophrenics not previously hospitalised to one of five groups. One received individual psychoanalytic-type psychotherapy, whilst a second was given *phenothiazine* drugs alone. The third was given a combination of psychotherapy and drugs, and the fourth ECT. The fifth received *milieu therapy*, a form of treatment that attempts to make a disturbed person's total environment a *therapeutic community*.

May's criteria of success were assessments of improvement made by nurses and clinicians, measures of 'release' rates, and the duration of hospitalisation. Drugs alone, and psychotherapy plus drugs, were the two most effective treatments. Since these two forms of treatment did not differ from one another, May concluded that psychotherapy had little or no tangible effects.

Faced with findings such as May's, it is tempting to conclude that some types of therapy *are* more effective than others. Despite methodological problems relating to their meta-analysis, Smith *et al.* (1980) argued that whilst all therapies produced beneficial changes, no particular type of therapy was significantly better than any other. A similar conclusion had been reached by Luborsky *et al.* (1975) some years earlier. Borrowing from Lewis Carroll's *Alice in Wonderland*, Luborsky *et al.* suggested that as far as effectiveness was concerned, 'everybody has won and all must have prizes'.

Box 6.5 *Explaining divergent findings about effectiveness*

Explaining the different conclusions about the relative effectiveness of therapies is difficult. However, one potential explanation is in terms of the measurements taken. As noted earlier, different therapies have different goals and therefore define 'improvement' in different ways. When an observable behaviour change is used as the criterion of success, behaviour therapy (which focuses on overt behaviour) is far superior to psychodynamic therapies (Shapiro & Shapiro, 1982). It could be argued that it would be much 'fairer' to examine the extent to which a therapy satisfies its *own* goals, but then there is the problem of whether everybody would consider the goals a therapeutic approach sets to be satisfactory ones.

Kiesler (1966) anticipated the problems outlined in Box 6.5 when he argued that the question, 'Which type of therapy is better?', is actually inappropriate. A much better question is:

'what type of treatment by what type of therapist is most effective in dealing with specific problems among specific persons?'.

Kiesler's question may be a more appropriate one, since it avoids the pitfalls of using *general outcome measures* which may mask differences between therapies, but it is also much more difficult to answer (Wilson & Barkham, 1994).

Do therapists influence a therapy's effectiveness?

Although they may practise the same therapeutic procedure, not all therapists are equally effective, implying that any benefits cannot be solely attributable to the therapy itself (Wolpe, 1985). Irrespective of the therapy they use, experienced therapists are generally (but not always) more effective than novice therapists (Russell, 1981). This suggests that therapists have something to learn, which means that therapeutic processes are not entirely futile (Carlson, 1988). One reason for experienced therapists' effectiveness is their willingness to embrace *technical eclecticism* or *multi-modal therapy*, in which techniques are borrowed from different therapies to tailor treatment to individual patients (Beitman *et al.*, 1989).

Experience alone, however, is not sufficient. With psychotherapy, research has consistently found that the most effective therapists genuinely care about those they treat, and aim to establish relationships which are empathic and foster respect and trust. By contrast, a lack of these qualities seems to be associated with *client deterioration*. As Truax & Carkhuff (1964) have observed:

> '[People] whose therapists offered a high level of unconditional positive warmth, self-congruence or genuineness, and empathic understanding showed significant positive personality and behaviour changes on a wide variety of indices, and ... [people] whose therapists offered relatively low levels of these conditions during therapy exhibited significant deterioration in personality and behaviour functioning' (see also Chapter 5).

The qualities described by Truax and Carkhuff are not, of course, exclusive to therapists. Strupp & Hadley (1979) asked university professors who were not professionally trained in psychotherapy, but were known to be warm, trustworthy and empathic, to 'treat' students experiencing depression and anxiety. Despite their lack of professional training, the professors were able to bring about a significant improvement in some students which was just as great as that produced in others by professional therapists.

Luborsky (1984) calls the ability to establish a warm and understanding relationship, in which the person seeking treatment and the person providing it believe they are working together, a *therapeutic alliance*. On the basis of Strupp and Hadley's findings, it seems that it is the therapeutic alliance, rather than a knowledge of psychopathology and its treatment, which is most important, at least for some disorders. The possibility that a treatment effect can be attributable solely to a therapist suggests that a therapy's effectiveness may have little more value than the *placebo effect*.

Box 6.6 *The placebo effect*

According to London (1964):

'Whatever is new and enthusiastically introduced and pursued seems, for the time, to work better than what previously did, whether or not it is more valid scientifically. Eventually, these novelties too join the Establishment of Techniques and turn out [to be] nothing more than went before'.

London was commenting on the fact that, in some cases, the mere belief or expectation that a treatment will be effective can be sufficient to convince a person that he or she has been helped, and thus to show signs of improvement. Shapiro (1971) has described the apparently successful use by faith healers and physicians centuries ago of drugs made from crocodile dung, human perspiration and pigs' teeth to treat illnesses they did not understand with ingredients that had no medicinal value.

Today, the media are constantly hailing *new* treatments as 'wonder cures', and it is possible that the therapeutic benefits associated with such cures are derived simply from the media attention they are given. To try to assess a therapy's effectiveness and overcome the placebo effect, researchers use *double blind control*. In this, the person administering the treatment *and* the person receiving it are kept ignorant as to the exact nature of the treatment being studied. Since neither knows what has actually been given, the expectations of both are minimised.

In studies assessing the effectiveness of drugs, the placebo treatment is an inert pill or injection. In psychotherapy, a person receiving a placebo is given relaxation therapy without any attempt to address the psychological problem. Achieving satisfactory double blind control is not always straightforward. For example, in studies of psychotherapeutic drugs, people can sometimes tell if they are receiving a placebo because of the *absence* of side-effects (see Chapter 1). However, this problem can be overcome by using *active placebos* which mimic a drug's side-effects but exert no other effect (Fisher & Greenberg, 1980).

Smith *et al.*'s (1980) meta-analytic study revealed that there was a significant placebo effect in therapy, confirming that when people *believe* they are receiving therapeutic attention, they tend to show some sort of improvement.

Does the type of disorder influence a therapy's effectiveness?

Some types of therapy are more effective for certain disorders. For example, drugs are essential in the treatment of schizophrenia, whereas psychodynamically based forms of therapy contribute little additional benefit (Pines, 1982). Behavioural treatments are significantly better than other approaches for treating agoraphobia (Berman & Norton, 1985). However, even *within* a therapeutic approach, differences have been observed. Recall from Chapter 3 that one type of behaviour therapy (flooding) is more effective than others (SD and implosion therapy) in the treatment of some phobias.

The meta-analytic studies described earlier also indicate that all therapies are not equally effective with different disorders. Amongst other things, Smith *et al.* (1980) found that whilst therapies derived from the psychodynamic model are effective, they are much more effective with anxiety disorders than with schizophrenia (see above). The rate of spontaneous remission has also been shown to vary considerably depending on the disorder. For example, people experiencing depression and GAD were more likely to recover spontaneously than those experiencing phobic or obsessive–compulsive disorders (Bergin & Lambert, 1978).

Does the type of person receiving therapy influence its effectiveness?

Some people have a choice about the sort of therapy they would prefer to undergo (Carlson, 1988). In at least some cases, then, people *self-select* a particular therapy. This makes it very difficult to assess therapies, because some people will either change therapists or leave therapy completely. As well as making it difficult to assess effectiveness, it makes comparisons between therapies difficult, since in both cases we are left with the evaluation *only* of those people who remain.

Despite this, some research findings should be mentioned. Garfield (1980) reported that therapies derived from the psychodynamic model are most effective with well-educated, articulate, strongly motivated and confident people experiencing light to moderate depression, anxiety disorders or interpersonal problems. Researchers call this the *YAVIS effect*, since such people tend to be **y**oung, **a**ttractive, **v**erbal, **i**ntelligent and **s**uccessful.

Also, since no two people will ever present *exactly* the same set of problems, no two people will ever receive exactly the same treatment. Precisely what will happen in a given therapeutic session is very hard to specify or assess even in those therapies (like behaviour therapy) where the therapist operates much more to a 'script' as far as the therapeutic session is concerned (Vallis *et al.*, 1986).

Box 6.7   *Culture and therapy*

At least some therapies *must* take into account the fact that people seeking treatment will come from diverse cultural or ethnic backgrounds. Rogler *et al.* (1987), for example, suggest that psychoanalysis or other therapies requiring high levels of verbal skills would be inappropriate for a person from a community whose members had completed little formal education.

In Hispanic societies, views concerning gender roles are different from those held by most members of Western societies. A therapeutic approach which did not take into account the established values and traditions of other cultures would lack *cultural sensitivity* and probably be of little benefit to a person seeking help (Baron, 1989).

Similarly, compared with American schizophrenics, Asian schizophrenics require significantly smaller amounts of neuroleptics for optimal treatment (Linn *et al.*, 1991). The reason for this is unclear, but it is likely that differences in metabolic rates, body fat and cultural practices (in, for example, eating) might be responsible.

Conclusions

Assessing the effectiveness of therapies and comparing their relative effectiveness is much more difficult than it might at first appear to be. The principal difficulty relates to measurement. Since there is no *criterion of success* which satisfies everybody, it is impossible to make judgements about effectiveness with which everyone would agree.

Summary

- Based on his assessment of psychoanalysis and eclectic psychotherapy, Eysenck concluded that neither was as effective as **no** treatment at all. Eysenck found that 66 per cent of people who had a similar problem to those who received therapy showed **spontaneous remission**. The cure/improvement figures for psychoanalysis and eclectic psychotherapy were 44 per cent and 64 per cent respectively.

- Eysenck's assessment has several methodological weaknesses, however. When the data are analysed using different measurements of 'improvement', the success rate for psychoanalysis increases dramatically. Eysenck's spontaneous remission figure has also been challenged.

- It is difficult to determine what the most appropriate **criterion for success** should be when trying to measure a therapy's effectiveness. Different therapies favour different measurements. Another issue concerns who determines whether a therapy has been effective. One approach is to use assessors who are not involved in the therapy being assessed.

- **Meta-analyses** look at all measurements of effectiveness in order to assess a therapy and combine the results of all research relating to it. This provides an 'average estimate' of the size of the therapy's effectiveness. Smith *et al.*'s meta-analysis indicated that psychodynamic therapies are effective, although some people show no improvement and a small percentage actually gets worse.

- Smith *et al.*'s meta-analysis has itself been criticised. When methodologically flawed studies are removed, Eysenck's original claim of no convincing evidence for psychotherapy's effectiveness is confirmed.

- Some studies comparing relative effectiveness indicate that therapies differ. Others indicate that no one type of therapy is significantly better than any other. One reason for these different conclusions is that improvement is defined in different ways. However, to ask 'Which type of therapy is better?' is inappropriate since it assumes 'general outcome measures', which may mask differences between therapies.

- Kiesler argues that it is much better to ask about the effectiveness of different therapies in relation to different therapists, different disorders, and different individuals. This, however, is a more complex question to answer.

- Not all therapists are equally effective, and experienced therapists are usually more effective than inexperienced ones. The possibility that a treatment may be effective solely because of the therapist suggests that a therapy's effectiveness may have little more value than the **placebo effect.**

- Some therapies are more effective for certain disorders. For example, drugs are essential in the treatment of schizophrenia, and behaviour therapies are significantly better than other approaches for the treatment of agoraphobia. Additionally, even within a therapeutic approach there may be differences. For example, flooding is more effective than SD and implosion therapy in treating some phobias.

- The type of person receiving a therapy also influences effectiveness. Psychodynamic therapies are most effective with well-educated, articulate, motivated and confident people with non-severe depression, anxiety disorders or interpersonal problems. Therapies must also consider the diversity of clients' cultural/ethnic backgrounds: they must display **cultural sensitivity** if they are to be of benefit.

ADAMS, H.E., TOLLISON, C.S. & CARSON, T.P. (1981) Behaviour therapy with sexual preventative medicine. In S.M. Turner, K.S. Calhoun & H.E. Adams (Eds) *Handbook of Clinical Behaviour Therapy*. New York: Wiley.

ANDREWS, G. (1991) The evaluation of psychotherapy. *Current Opinions of Psychotherapy*, 4, 379–383.

ANDREWS, G. (1993) The essential psychotherapies. *British Journal of Psychiatry*, 162, 447–451.

AYLLON, T. & AZRIN, N.H. (1968) *The Token Economy: A Motivational System for Therapy and Rehabilitation*. New York: Appleton Century Crofts.

AYLLON, T. & HAUGHTON, E. (1962) Control of the behaviour of schizophrenic patients by food. *Journal of the Experimental Analysis of Behaviour*, 5, 343–352.

BACHRACH, A., ERWIN, W. & MOHN, J. (1965) The control of eating behaviour in an anorexic by operant conditioning. In L. Ullman & L. Krasner (Eds) *Case Studies in Behaviour Modification*. New York: Holt, Rinehart & Winston.

BADDELEY, A.D (1997) *Human Memory: Theory and Practice* (revised edition). East Sussex: Psychology Press.

BANDURA, A. (1969) *Principles of Behaviour Modification*. New York: Holt, Rinehart & Winston.

BANDURA, A. (1971) *Social Learning Theory*. Morristown, NJ: General Learning Press.

BANDURA, A. (1977) *Social Learning Theory* (2nd edition). Englewood Cliffs, NJ: Prentice-Hall.

BARKER, P. (1998) The humanistic therapies. *Nursing Times*, 94, 52–53.

BARON, R.A. (1989) *Psychology: The Essential Science*. London: Allyn & Bacon.

BECK, A.T. (1967) *Depression: Causes and Treatment*. Philadelphia: University of Philadelphia Press.

BECK, A.T. & FREEMAN, A. (1990) *Cognitive Therapy of Personality Disorders*. New York: Guilford Press.

BECK, A.T., RUSH, A.J., SHAW, B.F. & EMORY, G. (1979) *Cognitive Therapy of Depression*. New York: Guilford Press.

BEITMAN, B., GOLDFRIED, M. & NORCROSS, J. (1989) The movement toward integrating the psychotherapies: An overview. *American Journal of Psychiatry*, 146, 138–147.

BENNETT, D. (1985) Rogers: More intuition than therapy. *APA Monitor*, 16, 3.

BENTON, D. (1981) Can the system take the shock? *Community Care*, 12 March, 15–17.

BERESFORD, D. (1997) Army gave gays shock treatment. *The Guardian*, 17 June, 13.

BERGIN, A.E. (1971) The evaluation of therapeutic outcomes. In A.E. Bergin & S.L. Garfield (Eds) *Handbook of Psychotherapy and Behaviour Change: An Empirical Analysis*. New York: Wiley.

BERGIN, A.E. (1980) Psychotherapy and religious values. *Journal of Consulting and Clinical Psychology*, 48, 642–645.

BERGIN, A.E. & LAMBERT, M.J. (1978) The evaluation of therapeutic outcomes. In S.A. Garfield & A.E. Bergin (Eds) *Handbook of Psychotherapy and Behaviour Change: An Empirical Analysis* (2nd edition). New York: Wiley.

BERMAN, J.S. & NORTON, N.C. (1985) Does professional training make a therapist more effective? *Psychological Bulletin*, 98, 401–407.

BERNE, E. (1964) *Games People Play: The Psychology of Human Relationships*. New York: Grove Press.

BERNE, E. (1976) *Beyond Games and Scripts*. New York: Grove Press.

BINI, L. (1938) Experimental researches on epileptic attacks induced by electric current. *American Journal of Psychiatry*, Supplement 94, 172–183.

BION, W.R. (1961) *Experiences in Groups*. London: Tavistock.

BNF (1997) *British National Formulary*. Number 32. London: British Medical Association/Royal Pharmaceutical Society of Great Britain.

BRANDSMA, J.M., MAULTSBY, M.C. & WELSH, R. (1978) 'Self-help techniques in the treatment of alcoholism.' Unpublished manuscript cited in G.T. Wilson & K.D. O'Leary *Principles of Behaviour Therapy*. Englewood Cliffs, NJ: Prentice-Hall.

BREGGIN, P. (1979) *Electroshock: Its Brain Disabling Effects*. New York: Springer.

BREGGIN, P. (1996) *Toxic Psychiatry*. London: Fontana.

BROCKNER, J. & GUARE, J. (1983) Improving the performance of low self-esteem individuals: An attributional approach. *Academy of Management Journal*, 29, 373–384.

BROWN, D. & ZINKIN, L. (1994) *The Psyche and the Social World: Developments in Group-Analytic Theory*. London: Routledge.

BURGESS, A. (1962) *A Clockwork Orange*. Harmandsworth: Penguin.

CARLSON, N.R. (1988) *Psychology: The Science of Behaviour*. London: Allyn & Bacon.

CAUTELA, J.R. (1967) Covert sensitisation. *Psychology Reports*, 20, 459–468.

CLARK, D.M. (1993) Treating panic attacks. *The Psychologist*, 6, 73–74.

CLARK, D.M., SALKOVSKIS, P.M., HACKMANN, A., MIDDLETON, H., ANASTASIADES, P. & GELDER, M. (1994) A comparison of cognitive therapy, applied relaxation and imipramine in the treatment of panic disorder. *British Journal of Psychiatry*, 164, 759–769.

COHN, H.W. (1994) What is existential psychotherapy? *British Journal of Psychiatry*, 165, 699–701.

CORNWELL, J. (1996) *The Power To Harm: Mind, Medicine and Murder on Trial*. New York: Viking.

COSTELLO, T.W., COSTELLO, J.T., & HOLMES, D.A. (Adapting author) (1995) *Abnormal Psychology*. London: HarperCollins.

COWART, J. & WHALEY, D.L. (1971) Punishment of self-mutilation behaviour. Cited in D.L. Whaley & R.W. Malott *Elementary Principles of Behaviour*. New York: Appleton Century Crofts.

CROOKS, R.L. & STEIN, J. (1991) *Psychology: Science, Behaviour and Life* (2nd edition). London: Holt, Rinehart & Winston Inc.

DAVID, A.S. (1994) Frontal lobology: Psychiatry's new pseudoscience. *British Journal of Psychiatry*, 161, 244–248.

DAVISON, G. & NEALE, J. (1994) *Abnormal Psychology* (6th edition). New York: Wiley.

DENKER, R. (1946) Results of treatment of psychoneuroses by the general practitioner: A follow-up study of 500 cases. *New York State Journal of Medicine*, 46, 356–364.

DOBSON, R. (1996) Confront your phobias in virtual reality. *The Sunday Times*, 21 January, 14.

DURHAM, R.C., MURPHY, J., ALLAN, T., RICHARD, K., TRELIVING, L.R. & FENTON, G.W. (1994) Cognitive therapy, analytic psychotherapy and anxiety management training for generalised anxiety disorder. *British Journal of Psychiatry*, 165, 315–323.

EISENBERG, I. (1995) The social construction of the human brain. *American Journal of Psychiatry*, 152, 1563–1575.

ELKINS, R.L. (1980) Covert sensitisation treatment of alcoholism. *Addictive Behaviours*, 5, 67–89.

ELLIS, A. (1958) *Rational Psychotherapy*. California: Institute for Rational Emotive Therapy.

ELLIS, A. (1962) *Reason and Emotion in Psychotherapy*. Secaucus, NJ: Lyle Stuart (Citadel Press).

ELLIS, A. (1984) Rational–emotive therapy. In R. Corsini (Ed.) *Current Psychotherapies* (3rd edition). Itasca, Il: Peacock.

ELLIS, A. (1991) The revised ABC of rational–emotive therapy. *Journal of Rational Emotive and Cognitive Behaviour Therapy*, 9, 139–192.

ELLIS, A. (1993) Reflections on rational–emotive therapy. *Journal of Consulting and Clinical Psychology*, 61, 199–201.

EMMELKAMP, P.M.G., BOUMAN, T.K. & SCHOLING, A. (1992) *Anxiety Disorders: A Practitioner's Guide*. New York: Plenum.

EMMELKAMP, P.M.G., KUIPERS, A.C.M. & EGGERAAT, J.B. (1978) Cognitive modification versus prolonged exposure *in vivo*: A comparison with agoraphobics as subjects. *Behaviour Research and Therapy*, 16, 33–42.

EYSENCK, H.J. (1952) The effects of psychotherapy: An evaluation. *Journal of Consulting Psychology*, 16, 319–324.

EYSENCK, H.J. (1965) The effects of psychotherapy. *International Journal of Psychiatry*, 1, 97–142.

EYSENCK, H.J. (1992) The outcome problem in psychotherapy. In W. Dryden & C. Feltham (Eds) *Psychotherapy and its Discontents*. Buckingham: Open University Press.

FAIRBURN, C.G., JONES, R. & PEVELER, R.C. (1993) Psychotherapy and bulimia nervosa: The longer-term effects of interpersonal psychotherapy, behaviour therapy and cognitive behaviour therapy. *Archives of General Psychiatry*, 50, 419–428.

FANCHER, R.T. (1995) *Cultures of Healing*. New York: W.H. Freeman.

FINK, M. (1984) Meduna and the origins of convulsive therapy in suicidal patients. *American Journal of Psychiatry*, 141, 1034–1041.

FISHER, S. & GREENBERG, R. (Eds) (1980) *A Critical Appraisal of Biological Treatments for Psychological Distress: Comparisons with Psychotherapy and Placebo*. Hillsdale, NJ: Erlbaum.

FORD, D.H. & URBAN, H.B. (1963) *Systems of Psychotherapy: A Comparative Study*. New York: Wiley.

FREEMAN, C. (Ed.) (1995) *The ECT Handbook*. London: Gaskell.

FREEMAN, H. & WATTS, J.W. (1942) *Psychosurgery*. Springfield, Ill.: Thomas.

FREUD, S. (1894) The defence neuropsychoses. In J. Strachey (Ed.) *The Standard Edition of the Complete Psychological Works of Sigmund Freud*, Volume 1. London: The Hogarth Press, 1953.

GARFIELD, S. (1980) *Psychotherapy: An Eclectic Approach*. New York: Wiley.

GARFIELD, S. (1992) Response to Hans Eysenck. In W. Dryden & C. Feltham (Eds) *Psychotherapy and its Discontents*. Buckingham: Open University Press.

GARFIELD, S. & BERGIN, A. (1994) Introduction and historical overview. In A. Bergin & S. Garfield (Eds) *Handbook of Psychotherapy and Behaviour Change*. Chichester: Wiley.

GARROD, A.B. (1859) *The Nature and Treatment of Gout and Rheumatic Gout*. London: Walton & Maberly.

GELDER, M., GATH, D. & MAYON, R. (1989) *The Oxford Textbook of Psychiatry* (2nd edition). Oxford: Oxford University Press.

GRAHAM, H. (1986) *The Human Face of Psychology*. Milton Keynes: Open University Press.

GREEN, S. (1996) Drugs and psychological disorders. *Psychology Review*, 3, 25–28.

GROSS R. & McILVEEN R. (1998) *Psychology: A New Introduction*. London: Hodder & Stoughton.

GUSCOTT, R. & TAYLOR, L. (1994) Lithium prophylaxis in recurrent affective illness: Efficacy, effectiveness and efficiency. *British Journal of Psychiatry*, 164, 741–746.

HAAGA, D.A. & DAVISON, G.C. (1993) An appraisal of rational-emotive therapy. *Journal of Consulting and Clinical Psychology*, 61, 215–220.

HAMILTON, L.W. & TIMMONS, C.R. (1995) Psychopharmacology. In D. Kimble & A.M. Colman (Eds) *Biological Aspects of Behaviour*. London: Longman.

HAY, P., SACHDEV, P. & CUMMING, S. (1993) Treatment of obsessive–compulsive disorder by psychosurgery. *Acta Psychiatrica Scandinavia*, 87, 197–207.

HEATHER, N. (1976) *Radical Perspectives in Psychology*. London: Methuen.

HERSHER, L. (Ed.) (1970) *Four Psychotherapies*. New York: Appleton-Century-Crofts.

HOLMES, J. (1996) Psychoanalysis – An endangered species? *Psychiatric Bulletin*, 20, 321–322.

HUTTON, A. (1998) Mental health: Drug update. *Nursing Times*, 94, February, 11.

ISAACS, W., THOMAS, J. & GOLDIAMOND, I. (1960) Application of operant conditioning to reinstate verbal behaviour in psychotics. *Journal of Speech and Hearing Disorders*, 25, 8–12.

JACOBSON, N.S., FOLLETTE, W.C. & REVENSTORF, D. (1984) Psychotherapy outcome research: Methods for reporting variability and evaluating clinical significance. *Behaviour Therapy*, 15, 336–352.

JAMES, I.A. & BLACKBURN, I.-M. (1995) Cognitive therapy with obsessive-compulsive disorder. *British Journal of Psychiatry*, 166, 144–150.

JOHNSTON, L. (1996) Move to outlaw electro therapy. *The Observer*, 12 December, 14.

JONES, M. C. (1924) The elimination of children's fears. *Journal of Experimental Psychology*, 7, 382–390.

KALINOWSKY, L. (1975) Psychosurgery. In A. Freedman, H. Kaplan & B. Sadock (Eds) *Comprehensive Textbook of Psychiatry*. Baltimore: Williams & Wilkins.

KEMPLER, W. (1973) Gestalt therapy. In R. Corsini (Ed.) *Current Psychotherapies*. Itasca, ILL: Peacock.

KIESLER, D.J. (1966) Some myths of psychotherapy research and the search for a paradigm. *Psychological Bulletin*, 65, 110–136.

KIPPER, D. (1992) Psychodrama: Group therapy through role playing. *International Journal of Group Psychotherapy*, 42, 495–521.

KREBS, D. & BLACKMAN, R. (1988) *Psychology: A First Encounter*. New York: Harcourt Brace Jovanovich.

LANDIS, C. (1938) Statistical evaluation of psychotherapeutic methods. In S.E. Hinde (Ed.) *Concepts and Problems of Psychotherapy*. London: Heineman.

LANGE, A.J. & JAKUBOWSKI, P. (1976) *Responsible Assertive Behaviour: Cognitive/Behavioural Procedures for Trainers*. Champaign, ILL: Research Press.

LAURANCE, J. (1993) Is psychotherapy all in the mind? *The Times*, 15 April, 7.

LAURENCE, C. (1997) Cheer up, son – take Prozac. *The Daily Telegraph*, 4 December, 27.

LEMONICK, M.D. (1997) The Mood Molecule. *Time*, September 29, 67–73.

LEVITSKY, A. & PERLS, F.S. (1970) The rules and games of Gestalt therapy. In J. Fagan & I. Shephard (Eds) *Gestalt Therapy Now*. Palo Alto, CA: Science and Behaviour Books.

LILIENFELD S.D. (1995) *Seeing Both Sides: Classic Controversies in Abnormal Psychology*. Pacific Grove: Brooks/Cole.

LINN, K.-M., MILLER, M.H., POLAND, R.E., NUCCIO, I. & YAMAGUCHI, M. (1991) Ethnicity and family involvement in the treatment of schizophrenic patients. *Journal of Nervous and Mental Disorder*, 179, 631–633.

LONDON, P. (1964) *The Modes and Morals of Psychotherapy*. New York: Holt, Rinehart & Winston.

LUBORSKY, L. (1984) *Principles of Psychoanalytic Psychotherapies: A Manual for Supportive–Expressive Treatment*. New York: Basic Books.

LUBORSKY, L., SINGER, B. & LUBORSKY, L. (1975) Comparative studies of psychotherapies: Is it true that 'everyone has won and all must have prizes'? *Archives of General Psychiatry*, 32, 49–62.

MacDONALD, V. (1996) Drug blunder resurfaces in children. *The Sunday Telegraph*, 15 December, 5.

MALAN, D.H., HEATH, E.S., BACAL, H.A. & BALFOUR, F.H.G. (1975) Psychodynamic changes in untreated neurotic patients. *Archives of General Psychiatry*, 32, 110–126.

MARKS, I. (1987) *Fears, Phobias and Rituals*. New York: Oxford University Press.

MASLOW, A. (1968) *Towards a Psychology of Being* (2nd edition). New York: Van Nostrand Reinhold.

MAY, P.R. (1975) A follow-up study of the treatment of schizophrenia. In R.L. Spitzer & D.F. Klein (Eds) *Evaluation of Psychological Therapies*. Baltimore: The Johns Hopkins University Press.

MEADOR, B.D. & ROGERS, C.R. (1973) Person-centred therapy. In R. Corsini (Ed.) *Current Psychotherapies*. Itasca, ILL: Peacock.

MEADOR, B.D. & ROGERS, C.R. (1984) Person-centred therapy. In R. Corsini (Ed.) *Current Psychotherapies* (3rd edition) Itasca, ILL: Peacock.

MEICHENBAUM, D.H. (1976) Towards a cognitive therapy of self-control. In G. Schawrtz & D. Shapiro (Eds) *Consciousness and Self-Regulation: Advances in Research*. New York: Plenum Publishing Co.

MEICHENBAUM, D.H. (1985) *Stress Inoculation Training*. New York: Pergamon.

MEICHENBAUM, D.H., HENSHAW, D. & HIMMEL, N. (1982) Coping with stress as a problem-solving process. In W. Krohne & L. Laux (Eds) *Achievement, Stress and Anxiety* . Washington, DC: Hemisphere.

MORENO, J.L. (1946) *Psychodrama*. New York: Beacon.

NIMH (1987) *The Switch Process in Manic-Depressive Illness* (DHHS Publication No. ADM 81–108). Washington, DC: Government Printing Office.

NSF (1994) *National Schizophrenia Fellowship: A Guide to the Types of Drugs Available to Treat Schizophrenia*. London: National Schizophrenia Fellowship.

OATLEY, K. (1984) *Selves in Relation: An Introduction to Psychotherapy and Groups*. London: Methuen.

PERLS, F.S. (1967) Group versus individual therapy. *ETC: A Review of General Semantics*, 34, 306–312.

PICCINELLI, M., PINI, S., BELLANTUONO, C. & WILKINSON, G. (1995) Efficacy of drug treatment in obsessive–compulsive disorder: A meta–analytic review. *British Journal of Psychiatry*, 166, 424–443.

PINES, M. (1982) Movement grows to create guidelines for mental therapy. *New York Times*, 4 May, C1, C6.

PRIOLEAU, L., MURDOCK, M. & BRODY, N. (1983) An analysis of psychotherapy versus placebo studies. *Behaviour and Brain Sciences*, 6, 273–310.

PROUDFOOT, J., GUEST, D., CARSON, J., DUNN, G. & GRAY, J. (1997) Effects of cognitive-behavioural training on job-find among long-term unemployed people. *Lancet*, 250, 96–100.

RABIN, A.S., KASLOW, N.J. & REHM, L.P. (1986) Aggregate outcome and follow-up results following self-control therapy for depression. Paper presented at the American Psychological Convention.

RAPPAPORT, Z.H. (1992) Psychosurgery in the modern era: Therapeutic and ethical aspects. *Medicine and Law*, 11, 449–453.

RASSOOL, G.H. & WINNINGTON, J. (1993) Using psychoactive drugs. *Nursing Times*, 89, 38–40.

RIMM, D.C. (1976) Behaviour therapy: Some general comments and a review of selected papers. In R.L. Spitzer & D.F. Klein (Eds) *Evaluation of Psychological Therapies*. Baltimore: Johns Hopkins University Press.

RIMM, D.C. & MASTERS, J.C. (1979) *Behaviour Therapy: Techniques and Empirical Findings* (2nd edition). New York: Academic Press.

ROBERTS, J.P. (1995) Group psychotherapy. *British Journal of Psychiatry*, 166, 124–129.

ROGERS, C.R. (1951) *Client-Centred Therapy: Its Current Practice, Implications and Theory*. Boston: Houghton-Mifflin.

ROGERS, C.R. (1973) My philosophy of interpersonal relationships and how it grew. *Journal of Humanistic Psychology*, 13, 3–16.

ROGERS, C.R. (1980) *A Way of Being*. Boston: Houghton-Mifflin.

ROGERS, C.R. (1986) Client-centred therapy. In I. Kutash & A. Wolf (Eds) *Psychotherapist's Casebook*. San Francisco: Jossey-Bass.

ROGERS, C.R. & DYMOND, R.F. (Eds) (1954) *Psychotherapy and Personality Change*. Chicago: University of Chicago Press.

ROGLER, L.H., MALGADY, R.G., CONSTANTINO, G. & BLUMENTHAL, R. (1987) What do culturally sensitive mental health services mean? The case of Hispanics. *American Psychologist*, 42, 565–570.

ROHSENOW, D.J. & SMITH, R.E. (1982) Irrational beliefs as predictors of negative affective states. *Motivation and Emotion*, 6, 299–301.

ROTH, A. & FONAGY, P. (1996) *Research on the efficacy and effectiveness of the psychotherapies: A report to the Department of Health*. London: HMSO.

RUSSELL, R. (1981) Report on effective psychotherapy: Legislative testimony. Paper presented at a public hearing on the Regulation of Mental Health Practitioners, New York (March).

SANE (1993) *Medical Methods of Treatment: A Guide to Psychiatric Drugs*. London: SANE Publications.

SCHNEIDER, B.H. & BYRNE, B.M. (1987) Individualising social skills training for behaviour-disordered children. *Journal of Consulting and Clinical Psychology*, 55, 444–445.

SHAPIRO, A.K. (1971) Placebo effects in medicine, psychotherapy and psychoanalysis. In A.E. Bergin & S.L. Garfield (Eds) *Handbook of Psychotherapy and Behaviour Change: An Empirical Analysis*. New York: Wiley.

SHAPIRO, D.A. & SHAPIRO, D. (1982) Meta-analysis of comparative therapy outcome studies: A replication and refinement. *Psychological Bulletin*, 92, 581–604.

SHARPE, M., HAWTON, K., SIMKIN, S., HACKMANN, A., KLIMES, I., PETO, T., WARRELL, S., & SEAGROAT, V. (1996) Cognitive-behavioural therapy for the chronic fatigue syndrome: A randomised controlled trial. *British Medical Journal*, 312, 22–26.

SHEAR, K.K., PILKONIS, P.A., CLOITRE, M. & LEON, A.C. (1994) Cognitive behavioural treatment compared with nonprescriptive treatment of panic disorders. *Archives of General Psychiatry*, 51, 395–401.

SILVERSTEIN, C. (1972) Behaviour modification and the gay community. Paper presented at the annual conference of the Association for the Advancement of Behaviour Therapy, New York.

SIMKIN, J.S. & YONTEF, G.M. (1984) Gestalt therapy. In R.J. Corsini (Ed.) *Current Psychotherapies* (3rd edition). Itasca, ILL: Peacock.

SLOANE, R., STAPLES, F., CRISTOL, A., YORKSTON, N. & WHIPPLE K. (1975) *Psychotherapy Versus Behaviour Therapy*. Cambridge MA: Harvard University Press.

SMITH, D. (1982) Trends in counselling and psychotherapy. *American Psychologist*, 37, 802–809.

SMITH, M.L., GLASS, G.V. & MILLER, T.I. (1980) *The Benefits of Psychotherapy*. Baltimore: Johns Hopkins University Press.

SNAITH, R.P. (1994) Psychosurgery: Controversy and enquiry. *British Journal of Psychiatry*, 161, 582–584.

STEVENSON, G.I. & BAKER, R. (1996) Brain Chemistry. *Education in Chemistry*, 33, 124–128.

STRUPP, H.H. & HADLEY, S.W. (1979) Specific versus non-specific factors in psychotherapy: A controlled study of outcome. *Archives of General Psychiatry*, 36, 1125–1136.

TALLIS, R. (1996) Burying Freud. *The Lancet*, 347, 669–671.

TARRIER, N., BECKETT, R. & HARWOOD, S. (1993) A trial of two cognitive behavioural methods of treating drug-resistant residual psychotic symptoms in schizophrenic patients. *British Journal of Psychiatry*, 162, 524–532.

THOMAS, K. (1990) Psychodynamics: The Freudian approach. In I. Roth (Ed.) *Introduction to Psychology*. Hove: Lawrence Erlbaum Associates Ltd.

THORNE, B. (1984) Person-centred therapy. In W. Dryden (Ed.) *Individual Therapy in Britain*. London: Harper Row.

TRUAX, C.B. (1966) Reinforcement and non-reinforcement in Rogerian therapy. *Journal of Abnormal Psychology*, 71, 1–9.

TRUAX, C.B. & CARKHUFF, R.R. (1964) Significant developments in psychotherapy research. In L.E. Abt & B.F. Reiss (Eds) *Progress in Clinical Psychology*. New York: Grune & Stratton.

VALENSTEIN, E.S. (1973) *Brain Control*. New York: John Wiley and Sons.

VALENSTEIN, E.S. (1980) Rationale and psychosurgical procedures. In E.S. Valenstein (Ed.) *The Psychosurgery Debate*. San Francisco: W.H. Freeman.

VALENSTEIN, E.S. (1990) The prefrontal area and psychosurgery. *Progress in Brain Research*, 85, 539–554.

VALLIS, M., McCABE, S.B. & SHAW, B.F. (1986) The relationships between therapist skill in cognitive therapy and general therapy skill. Paper presented to the Society for Psychotherapy Research, Wellesley, MA. (June).

VERKAIK, R. (1995) The kindest cut of all? *The Sunday Times*, 30 July, 18–19.

WALKER, S. (1984) *Learning Theory and Behaviour Modification*. London: Methuen.

WATSON, J.B. & RAYNER, R. (1920) Conditioned emotional responses. *Journal of Experimental Psychology*, 3, 1–14.

WEBSTER, R. (1995) *Why Freud was Wrong: Sin, Science and Psychoanalysis*. London: HarperCollins.

WESSELEY, S. (1993) Shocking treatment. *The Times*, 18 November, 22.

WILLIAMS, J.M.G. (1992) *The Psychological Treatment of Depression*. London: Routledge.

WILSON, G.T. & O'LEARY, K.D. (1978) *Principles of Behaviour Therapy*. Englewood Cliffs, NJ: Prentice-Hall.

WILSON, J.E. & BARKHAM, M. (1994) A practitioner-scientist approach to psychotherapy process and outcome research. In P. Clarkson & M. Pokorny (Eds) *The Handbook of Psychotherapy*. London: Routledge.

WILSON, P. (1982) Combined pharmacological and behavioural treatment of depression. *Behaviour Research and Therapy*, 20, 173–184.

WINTER, A. (1972) Depression and intractible pain treated by modified prefrontal lobotomy. *Journal of Medical Sociology*, 69, 757–759.

WOLPE, J. (1958) *Psychotherapy by Reciprocal Inhibition*. Stanford, CA: Stanford University Press.

WOLPE, J. (1973) *The Practice of Behaviour Therapy*. New York: Pergamon Press.

WOLPE, J. (1985) Existential problems and behaviour therapy. *The Behaviour Therapist*, 8, 126–127.

WOLPE, J. & WOLPE, D. (1981) *Our Useless Years*. Boston: Houghton-Mifflin.

INDEX

A-B-C model (Ellis) 56–9
acrophobia 37–8
acting out **25**
active interpretation **73**
active listening **72**
Adams, H.E. 42
addiction
  alcohol 6
  opiate 6
agoraphobia 3, 60, 78, 97
agranulocytosis 2–3
akathisia 2
alcohol
  abuse 42–3
  addiction 6
Alice in Wonderland 93
amnesia (following ECT) 10
  anterograde 10
  retrograde 10
amphetamine abuse 2
amplification (in Gestalt therapy)
  79, 80
analysand 19, 20, 21, 22, 23, 25,
  31
Andrews, G. 63, 66, 92
anorexia nervosa 46–7
antianxiety drugs (*see* anxiolytics)
antidepressants and antimanics 1,
  3–6, 10, 93
  monoamine oxidase inhibitors
    (MAOIs) 3, 4
  tetracyclics (selective serotonin
    reuptake inhibitors) 3–4
  tricyclics 3, 4
antipsychotics (*see* neuroleptics)
anxiety 3, 6, 7, 28, 37, 43, 66,
  95, 97
  see also generalised anxiety

  disorder
  hierarchy 38, 39
  management training 89
anxiolytics (antianxiety drugs,
  minor tranquillisers) 6–7
  barbiturates 6
  benzodiazepine group 6
  propanediol group 6
application and follow-through 66
arachnophobia 40
assertiveness training 56
atropine sulphate 8
attributional therapy 53, **63**–4
atypical neuroleptics 2, 3
authenticity (*see* genuineness)
auxiliary egos 28–9
aversion therapy 36, **40**–2
Ayllon, T. 47–8
Azrin, N.H. 47–8
Bachrach, A. 46–7
Baddeley, A.D. 49
Baker, R. 4
Bandura, A. 53, 54–6, 76
barbiturates (phenobarbitone) 6
Barker, P 76
Barkham, M. 94
Baron, R.A. 98
basic rule (of psychoanalysis) 20
Beck, A.T. 53, 61–3
bedwetting (*see* nocturnal
  enuresis)
behaviour modification
  techniques 35, 43– 49, 50
  behaviour shaping and 42, **46**–7
  extinction as 43, 44
  issues in 49–50
  positive reinforcement as 43,
    46–49

punishment as 45
behaviour therapy 35–43, 49–50, 88, 89
  aversion therapy 36, 40–2
  covert sensitisation (CS) 36, **42**–3
  flooding **36**–7, 40, 97
  implosion therapy 36, **37**, 50, 97
  issues in 49–50
  systematic desensitisation (SD) 36, 38, **39**–40, 97
behavioural rehearsal 56
Beitman, B. 94
Bennett, D. 70
Benton, D. 10
benzodiazepines (chlordiazepoxide, diazepam) 6, 7
Beresford, D. 41
Bergin, A.E. 26, 61, 86, 97
Berman, J.S. 97
Berne, E. 29–31
Bini, L. 8
Bion, W.R. 28
bipolar disorder **5**, 9
Blackburn, I.-M. 67
Blackman, R. 87, 88
BNF 3
Brandsma, J.M. 61
Breggin, P. 4, 11
Brockner, J. 64
Brown, D. 28
Burgess, A. 41
Busparin 7
butyrophenones (droperidol, haloperidol) 2
Byrne, B.M. 49
Camoclit (*see* lithium carbonate)

capsulotomies **15**
carbon dioxide inhalation therapy 1
Cardiazol 7–8
Carkhuff, R.R. 95
Carlson, N.R. 8, 10, 94, 97
Carroll, Lewis 93
Cautela, J.R. 43
chemotherapy 1–7, 13, 92, 93, 96
  antidepressants and antimanics 1, 3–6, 10
  anxiolytics (anti-anxiety drugs, minor tranquillisers) 6–7
  neuroleptics (antipsychotics, major tranquillisers) 1–3
chlordiazepoxide (Librium) 6
chlorpromazine (Largactil, Thorazine) 2
chronic fatigue syndrome 67
cingulotomy 14, **15**
cingulum bundle 15
Clark, D.M. 66, 67
classical conditioning 35–43, 54
client- (or person-) centred therapy 69–76, 79
  application and evaluation of 73–6
  empathy (empathic understanding) in **71**–2, 73, 95
  encouraging personal growth in 70–2
  genuineness (authenticity, congruence) in **70**–1, 72, 95
  Q-sorts and 75
  unconditional positive regard in **71**, 72, 76, 95
client deterioration 95

Clockwork Orange, A 41
closed system (psychoanalysis as) 32
clozapine (Clozaril) 2
Clozaril (*see* clozapine)
cognitive preparation (conceptualisation) 64
cognitive restructuring therapy 53, 61–3
  cognitive triad **61**
  effectiveness of 63
cognitive therapies 53–68, 89
  attributional therapy 53, 63–4
  cognitive restructuring therapy 53, 61–3
  rational–emotive therapy (RET) 53, 56–61, 63
  stress-inoculation therapy 53, 64–6
cognitive–behavioural therapies 53–6
  assertiveness training 56
  modelling **54**–5
  social-skills training 56
cognitive triad **61**
Cohn, H.W. 27
conceptualisation (*see* cognitive preparation)
conduct disorders 49
confrontation (in psychoanalysis) 23
congruence (*see* genuineness)
Cornwell, J. 4
Costello, T.W. 5
countertransference **24**
covert sensitisation (CS) 36, **42**–3, 54
Cowart, J. 45
criterion of success (in therapy) 87, 99
Crooks, R.L. 44, 87
CS (*see* covert sensitisation)
cultural sensitivity 98
David, A.S. 1, 14
Davison, G. 15, 61
defence mechanisms 26
Denker, R. 86
depressants 6
depression (unipolar disorder) 3–5, 9, 10, 15, 25, 57, 61, 62, 63, 64, 67, 95, 97
dialogue (in Gestalt therapy) 79
diazepam (Valium) 6
dibezazepines 2
dispute belief system **57**
dissocial personality disorder 76
Dobson, R. 38
dopamine 2
dose–effect relationship **90**
double blind control **96**
doubling (in psychodrama) 29
dream interpretation 19
Droleptan (*see* droperidol)
droperidol (Droleptan) 2
drug holidays (*see* targeted strategies)
Durham, R.C. 89
Dymond, R.F. 75
dystonia 2
eating disorders 3, 46–7, 63
eclectic psychotherapy **85**
ECT (*see* electroconvulsive therapy)
Edronax (*see* reboxetine)
ego 18, 19, 20, 26, 27, 30
ego analysts (*see* ego psychologists)
ego psychologists (ego analysts) 27

ego states (in transactional
    analysis) 29–30
  adult state 30
  child state 29
  parent state 29
Eisenberg, I. 18
electroconvulsive therapy (ECT)
    1, 7–11, 93
  bilateral **8**
  biochemical changes in 10
  effectiveness of 10–11
  ethical issues and 10–11
  frequency of treatments 9
  procedures in 8–9
  sub-convulsive shocks in 10
  unilateral 8
Elkins, R.L. 59
Ellis, A. 53, 56–61
Emmelkamp, P.M.G. 37, 40, 60
empathic understanding (*see*
    empathy)
empathy (empathic
    understanding) 61, **71**–2, 95
empty chair exercise 79
encounter groups 81
epilepsy 7
extinction (as behaviour
    modification technique) **43**,
    44
extrapyramidal symptoms 2
  akathisia 2
  dystonia 2
  tardive dyskinesia 2
Eysenck, H.J. 85–9, 91, 92
facilitator 81
Fairburn, C.G. 63
Fancher, R.T. 61
Fink, M. 7
Fisher, S. 96

flooding **36**–7, 40, 97
fluoxetine (Prozac) 3, 4–5
focal psychotherapies **26**–7
Fonagy, P. 28
Ford, D.H. 21
free association **20**–3
Freeman, A. 63
Freeman, C. 9
Freeman, H. 13
Freud, Anna 27
Freud, S. 18, 19–20, 22–5, 27,
    31, 76–7, 85–7
Freudian slips (*see* parapraxes)
GAD (*see* generalised anxiety
    disorder)
Garfield, S. 26, 92, 98
Garrod, A.B. 5
Gelder, M. 40
generalised anxiety disorder
    (GAD) 6, 89, 97
genuineness (authenticity,
    congruence) **70**–1, 72, 73, 95
Gestalt therapy **76**–80, 82
  effectiveness and
    appropriateness of 80
  moral injunctions of 80
  organismic self-regulation and
    78
  techniques in 78–80
gouty mania 5
Graham, H. 81
Green, S. 3
Greenberg, R. 96
Gross, R. 62, 63
group psychotherapy 28–31
Guare, J. 64
Guscott, R. 87
Haaga, D.A. 61
Hadley, S.W. 95

Haldol (*see* haloperidol)
haloperidol (Haldol) 2
Hamilton, L.W. 3
Haughton, E. 47
Hay, P. 15
Heather, N. 10
Hersher, L. 75
Holmes, J. 18, 26, 28
homosexuality 41–2
humanistic therapies 69–84
    client- (or person-) centred
        therapy 69–76, 79
    encounter groups 81
    Gestalt therapy 76–80, 82
    sensitivity training groups (T-
        groups) 81–2
Hutton, A. 3
hypnosis 19
hypothalamus 2, 12, 15
id 18, 27, 30
imipramine (Tofranil) 3
implosion therapy **36**, 37, 40, 97
insight **19**, 25–6, 31–2
insulin coma therapy 1
interactions
    complementary 30
    crossed 30
interpretation of faulty actions (in
    psychoanalysis) **19**
interpretation of physiological
    cues (in psychoanalysis) 19
interpretive comments (in
    psychoanalysis) 22
irrational beliefs 56, 57–8, 59, 61
Isaacs, W. 46
Jacobson, N.S. 89
Jakubowski, P. 59
James, I.A. 67
Johnston, L. 9

Jones, M.C. 38
Kalinowsky, L. 13
Kemadrin (*see* procyclidine)
Kempler, W. 78
Kiesler, D.J. 94
Kipper, D. 29
Krebs, D. 87, 88
Lambert, M.J. 97
Landis, C. 86, 87
Lange, A.J. 59
Largactil (*see* chlorpromazine)
latent content (of dreams) **19**
Laurance, J. 18
Laurence, C. 5
learned helplessness **63**
Lemonick, M.D. 4
leucotomy (*see* pre-frontal
    lobotomy)
Levitsky, A. 78
Librium (*see* chlordiazepoxide)
Lilienfeld, S.D. 10, 90
limbic system 15
Linn, K.-M. 98
Liskanum (*see* lithium carbonate)
Litarex (*see* lithium citrate)
lithium carbonate (Camoclit,
    Liskanum) 5
lithium salts (Litarex, Piradel) 5–6
lobotomy 12–13
    pre-frontal 12–13
    transorbital 13
London, P. 96
Luborsky, L. 90, 93, 95
MacDonald, V. 7
major tranquillisers (*see*
    neuroleptics)
Malan, D.H. 86
malaria therapy 1
mania 2, 5

manifest content (of dreams) **19**
MAOI antidepressants (*see*
    monoamine oxidase inhibitor
    antidepressants)
Marks, I. 40
Maslow, A. 82
Masters, J.C. 50, 80
May, P.R. 93
McIlveen, R. 62, 63
Meador, B.D. 69, 70
Meichenbaum, D.H. 53, 64–6
meprobamate (Miltown) 6
meta-analysis **90**–2, 96, 97
milieu therapy **93**
Miltown (*see* meprobamate)
minor tranquillisers (*see*
    anxiolytics)
mirroring (in psychodrama) 29
modelling **54**–6
    participant 54–5
    symbolic 54
models 54
monoamine oxidase inhibitor
    antidepressants (MAOI
    antidepressants) 3, 4
Moreno, J.L. 28–9
multi-modal therapy (*see* technical
    eclecticism)
narcosis therapy 1
Nardil (*see* phenelzine)
Neale, J. 86
neuroleptic malignant syndrome 2
neuroleptics (antipsychotics,
    major tranquillisers) 1–3, 98
    atypical 2, 3
    butyrophenones 2
    dibezazepines 2
    phenothiazines 2
NIMH 5

nitrogen shock therapy 1
nocturnal enuresis (bedwetting) 5
non-directive therapy 69
noradrenaline 4, 5
Norton, N.C. 97
NSF 3
O'Leary, K.D. 40
Oatley, K. 86
object relations theorists **27**
observational learning 54
obsessive–compulsive disorder
    (OCD) 3, 9, 15, 67, 92, 93,
    97
OCD (*see* obsessive–compulsive
    disorder)
olanzapine (Zyprexa) 3
operant conditioning 35, 42,
    43–9, 54
organismic self-regulation 78
pain 11, 66
    control 14
panic disorder 66–7
parapraxes (*see* interpretation of
    faulty actions)
Perls, F.S. 69, 76–80, 82
personality disorders 63
phenelzine (Nardil) 3
phenobarbitol 6
phenothiazines (*see*
    chlorpromazine) 2, 93
phobic behaviour 36, 37–8
phobic disorders 54, 55, 87, 97
Piccinelli, M. 92–3
Pines, M. 97
Piradel (*see* lithium citrate)
placebo 92
placebo effect 95–6
planned experiences (in Gestalt
    therapy) 76

positive reinforcement (as behaviour modification technique) 46–9
  behaviour shaping 42, 46–7
  token economy system 47–9
pre-frontal lobotomy (leucotomy) **12**
Prioleau, L. 92
private deduction (in psychoanalysis) 23
procyclidine (Kemadrin) 2
propanediols (meprobamate) 6
protagonist in psychodrama) 28–9
Proudfoot, J. 67
Prozac (*see* fluoxetine)
psychoanalysis 18, **19**–26, 31–2, 56, 76, 78, 85–7, 98
  as a closed system 32
  techniques used in 19–26
psychoanalyst 18, 56, 58, 87–8
psychoanalytically oriented psychotherapies 26
  focal psychotherapies 26–7
psychodrama 28–9
psychodynamic therapies 18–34, 35, 91–3, 94
  group psychotherapy 28–31
  issues concerning 31–2
  psychoananalysis 18, 19–26, 31–2, 85–7
  psychoanalytically oriented psychotherapies 26–7
  psychotherapy 28–31, 85, 88, 89, 90, 93, 96
psychosurgery 1, 11–15
  capsulotomies **15**
  cingulotomy 14, 15
  consent in 14

consistency and irreversibility of 14
  lack of evaluation in 14
  lack of scientific basis in 14
  pre-frontal lobotomy (leucotomy) **12**–13, 14
  side-effects of 14
  tractotomy **15**
  transorbital lobotomy **13**
psychotherapeutic drugs (*see* chemotherapy)
psychotherapy
  eclectic **85**
  effectiveness of 85–93, 96
  focal **26**–7
  group 28–31
  issues in 88, 89, 90, 93, 95
  psychoanalytically oriented 26
punishment (as behaviour modification technique) 45
  effectiveness and ethics of 45
Q-sorts **75**
Rabin, A.S. 64
Rappoport, Z.H. 14
Rassool, G.H. 7
rational–emotive therapy (RET) 56–61
  A-B-C model and 56–9
  dispute belief system 57
  effectiveness of 60–1
  irrational beliefs and 56, 57–8, 59
Rayner, R. 35
rebound anxiety **6**–7
reboxetine (Edronax) 4
recidivism rates **90**
reciprocal inhibition **39**
reconstruction (in psychoanalysis) 23

reflection 73
reinforcing self-statements 65–6
relaxation training 38–9
resistance (in psychoanalysis) **22**, 32
response disinhibition **54**
response inhibition 54
RET (*see* rational–emotive therapy)
Rimm, D.C. 50, 80
Risperdal (*see* risperidone)
risperidone (Risperdal) 3
Roberts, J.P. 28
Rogers, C.R. 69–76, 79, 81
Rogler, L.H. 98
Rohsenow, D.J. 58
role playing (in Gestalt therapy) 79
role reversal (in psychodrama) 29, 30
Roth, A. 28
Russell, R. 94
SANE 1
schizophrenia 2, 3, 7, 9, 12, 25, 46, 47–8, 61, 63, 76, 93, 97, 98
   negative symptoms in 3
   positive symptoms in 3
Schneider, B.H. 49
SD (*see* systematic desensitisation)
selective serotonin reuptake inhibitors (*see* tetracyclic antidepressants)
self-efficacy **56**
self-serving bias **63**–4
sensitivity training groups (T-groups) 81–2
serotonin 4, 5
Shapiro, D. 92, 94

Shapiro, D.A. 92, 94
Sharpe, M. 67
Shear, K.K. 67
Silverstein, C. 42
Simkin, J.S. 80
skill acquisition and rehearsal 64
Sloane, R. 88, 89
Smith, D. 18
Smith, M.L. 90–2, 93, 96, 97
Smith, R.E. 58
Snaith, R.P. 15
social learning theorists **54**
social skills training **56**
somatic therapy 1–17
   carbon dioxide inhalation therapy 1
   chemotherapy 1–7
   electroconvulsive therapy (ECT) 1, 7–11
   insulin coma therapy 1
   malaria therapy 1
   narcosis therapy 1
   nitrogen shock therapy 1
   psychosurgery 1, 11–15
sounding board (psychoanalyst as) 21
speaking in the first person (in Gestalt therapy) 79–80
spontaneous remission **85–6**, 87, 89
SSRIs (*see* tetracyclic antidepressants)
Stein, J. 44, 87
Stevenson, G.I. 4
stimulants 3
stimulus augmentation **35**
stress inoculation therapy 53, 64–6
   application and follow-through

66
cognitive preparation
(conceptualisation) 64
effectiveness of 66
reinforcing self-statements
65–6
skill acquisition and rehearsal
64
Strupp, H.H. 95
superego 18, 30
symptom substitution **49**
systematic desensitisation (SD)
36, 38, **39**–40, 54, 97
T-groups (*see* sensitivity training
groups)
Tallis, R. 31
tardive dyskinesia **2**
target behaviours 47–8
targeted strategies (drug holidays)
2
Tarrier, N. 63
Taylor, L. 87
technical eclecticism (multi-modal
therapy) 94
tetracyclic antidepressants
(selective serotonin reuptake
inhibitors) 3–4
thalamus 12
thanatophobia 39
therapeutic alliance **95**
therapeutic community **93**
therapist bias 87
Thomas, K. 24
Thorazine (*see* chlorpromazine)
Thorne, B. 73
Timmons, C.R. 3
Tofranil (*see* imipramine)
token economy system **47**–9
issues concerning 49

tractotomy **15**
training analysis 24
transactional analysis 28, 29–31
transference (transference
neurosis) 23–5
transference neurosis (*see*
transference)
transorbital lobotomy **13**
tricyclic antidepressants
(imipramine) 3, 4
Truax, C.B. 75, 95
unconditional positive regard **71**,
72, 76, 95
unemployment 67
unipolar disorder (*see* depression)
uproar (in transactional analysis)
30
Urban, H.B. 21
urinary retention 5
Valenstein, E.S. 13, 14, 15
Valium (*see* diazepam)
Vallis, M. 98
Verkaik, R. 15
virtual reality (as treatment for
phobias) 37–8
visual imagery 54
Walker, S. 35
Watson, J.B. 35
Watts, J.W. 13
Webster, R. 31
Wesseley, S. 9–10
Whaley, D.L. 45
Williams, J.M.G. 63
Wilson, G.T. 40
Wilson, J.E. 94
Wilson, P 54
Winnington, J. 7
Winter, A. 14
wish fulfilment 19

Wolpe, D. 39
Wolpe, J. 36–7, 38, 39, 94
working through **25–6**
YAVIS effect **98**

Yontef, G.M. 80
Zinkin, L. 28
Zopiclone 7
Zyprexa (*see* olanzapine)